THE INSIDER'S GUIDE TO

THAILAND

THE INSIDER'S GUIDES
JAPAN • CHINA • KOREA • HONG KONG • BALI • THAILAND • INDIA • NEPAL • AUSTRALIA
HAWAII • CALIFORNIA • NEW ENGLAND • FLORIDA • MEXICO
THE SOVIET UNION • SPAIN • TURKEY • GREECE
KENYA • INDONESIA

The Insider's Guide to Thailand
First Published 1989
Second Edition 1991

Moorland Publishing Co Ltd
Moor Farm Rd., Airfield Estate, Ashbourne, DE6 1HD, England
By arrangement with Novo Editions

© 1989, 1991 Novo Editions

ISBN: 0 86190 448 6

Created, edited and produced by Novo Editions
53 rue Beaudouin, Les Andelys, France. Fax: (33) 32 54 54 50
Editor in Chief: Allan Amsel
Original design concept: Hon Bing-wah
Picture editor and designer: Leonard Lueras
Text and artwork composed and information updated
using Xerox Ventura software

ACKNOWLEDGMENTS
The Author would like to acknowledge the kind assistance given him by many people,
but particularly by Aroonsri Srimekhanond and Rungsan Tanvisuth, both of
the Tourism Authority of Thailand.

Printed by Samhwa Printing Co Ltd, Seoul, Korea

THE INSIDER'S GUIDE TO

THAILAND

by Bradley Winterton

Photographed by Nik Wheeler

MPC

Contents

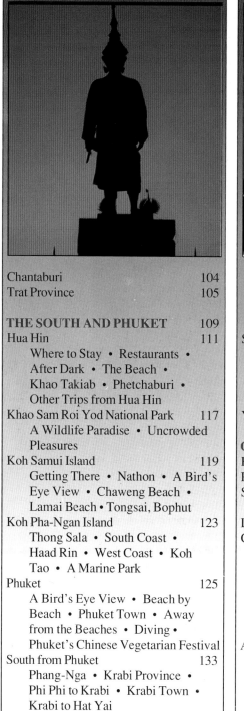

THAILAND

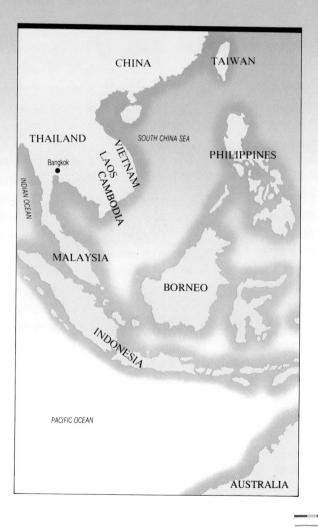

CHINA

TAIWAN

THAILAND

SOUTH CHINA SEA

Bangkok

VIETNAM

LAOS

CAMBODIA

PHILIPPINES

INDIAN OCEAN

MALAYSIA

BORNEO

INDONESIA

PACIFIC OCEAN

AUSTRALIA

Railways
Roads

50 km

The Siamese World

A VERY SPECIAL PLACE

Thailand is like nowhere else in Asia. Although for centuries its Buddhism and its social organisation made it not unlike the neighbouring territories of Burma, Cambodia and Vietnam, today it is unique.

Whereas Malaysia to the south is Islamic and federal, and the countries to the north and east are under the sway of variously totalitarian regimes, Thailand continues to display the traditional styles of a Buddhist monarchy. And despite or because of this, it is currently experiencing a period of unrivalled economic expansion.

Thailand is a country that's changing fast. But it remains so colorful, so easy-going, and so welcoming that there are few more attractive tourist destinations anywhere in Asia.

What, then, are the key elements of this unique and special place?

A PINK ELEPHANT

To some observers, the land of Thailand resembles the head and trunk of an elephant, the animal for so long symbolic of the country and for a time featured, colored pink, on its national flag.

The country extends northward from the Malaysian border up a long, narrow isthmus before broadening out just south of Bangkok into a wide, low-lying plain. This, the delta of the Chao Phraya river, constitutes the Thai heartland. Westwards the land rises to the high hills that eventually become the border with Burma, while to the east a coastal plain runs down to the frontier with Cambodia. Meanwhile, in the northeast the land rises slightly to become the sandstone plain that extends to the banks of the Mekong river, and this river for a considerable distance forms part of Thailand's long border with Laos. The far north is rugged, and Chiang Mai, Thailand's second city, is situated in the only

important level area. The country has no common border with China.

From south to north Thailand measures just over 1,600 km (1,000 miles), and a train journey from Hat Yai near the Malaysian border to Chiang Mai at the northern end of the country's rail system would take a good 36 hours. East to west, Thailand extends 786 km (485 miles) at its widest, just north of Bangkok.

The population of 49 million is distributed unevenly, with the greatest concentration in the central rice-growing area and

the sparsest in the northern and southern hills.

A HOT CLIMATE

Thailand's climate is classically tropical, though not equatorial. The country experiences three seasons — a cool, dry season from November to January, a hot and dry season from February to May, and a rainy season from June to October. The dry season winds blow out of the northeast, from China, while the rain-bearing winds ("monsoons") blow in from the Indian Ocean to the southwest.

The length, strength and constancy of the rains vary from year to year. Whereas this constitutes a nuisance in the low-lying river basins when heavy deluges lead to flooding (an annual occurrence in Bangkok), the more serious problems come in the northeast which, lacking the irrigation systems of the great river valleys, is totally dependent on the annual rains. Here, if the rains are unsatisfactory, crop failure and consequent rural depopulation are an ever-present threat.

Two versions of tropical promise – OPPOSITE: Pattaya sunset; ABOVE: Bangkok's Wat Arun, Temple of the Dawn.

This rainfall pattern is different in the south of the country. Here the seasons begin to be influenced by the more equatorial climate of the Malaysian peninsula. Rain is experienced in most months of the year, and in December and January, two of the driest months in the rest of the country, it can be particularly heavy.

Temperatures, by contrast, are remarkably constant throughout the country, rarely going above 35°C or below 18°C (96° and 65°F). Cooler temperatures, though, are

Yunnan Province of China (the area immediately north of Vietnam and Laos, and east of Burma). Some scholars believe the Thais are a branch of the Chinese race, others that their culture existed as a separate entity before the Chinese themselves arrived in the Yunnan area.

Whichever is true, the Thais certainly established a distinctive kingdom in the seventh century in Yunnan called Nanchao, and for two hundred years competed with the Chinese for control of the territory.

experienced in the northern hills, especially at night in December and January. What is really to the advantage of the north, however, is its lower humidity: it is the consistently high humidity of Bangkok and the south generally that makes the climate trying for many visitors from temperate regions.

The Chinese eventually overcame them, and from then on, it seems, the Thais began to migrate southwards into modern Burma, modern Laos and the northern part of modern Thailand. Since then they've never looked back.

ENTER THE THAIS

WHERE DO THEY COME FROM?

The Thais belong to a racial group that includes the Shans of Burma, the Lao of Laos, and Thai-speaking inhabitants of the

OLD SIAM

THE SUKHOTHAI PERIOD

The great power in the region at this time was the Khmer Empire, based in modern Cambodia, and in the thirteenth century the Thai princelings buried their differences and challenged the Khmers in their local garrison of Sukhothai. They won, and founded their first capital on modern Thai soil on the same site in 1238.

There is little doubt that the Thais couldn't have overcome such a major power on their own. Aid almost certainly came from the Chinese who were more than willing to support anyone who might lessen the influence of the great Khmer Empire on their southern flank. As for the Burmese, who might be expected to have resisted the

establishment of a new kingdom on their borders, they were already occupied fighting off the Mongols.

The Thais found a powerful leader in these Sukhothai years in King Ramkamheng (1283–1317). Not only did he hold off the Khmers — he also extended Thai control down the valley of the Chao Phraya River (on which Bangkok stands), and commissioned scholars to create for the first time a written form for the Thai language.

Trade flourished early between the new state and its patron both by land and, once the Thais had established themselves on the coast of the Gulf of Siam, by sea. Chinese ceramicists came to Sukhothai and taught

the locals the art of potting. This good relationship with China was to last nearly six hundred years.

Nations in those days were little more than areas over which families, and alliances between families, held control, and after the death of King Ramkamheng decline set in. Rival centers of strength became established in the more fertile south, and by the middle of the fourteenth century, Ayutthaya had established itself as the power-base of the dominant Thai faction. It wasn't long before Sukhothai was forced to accept the supremacy of the new capital.

NARESUAN THE GREAT

Over the centuries that followed, Ayutthaya became immensely powerful, extending its control into the south of modern Burma as far as the Bay of Bengal, and down into the Malay peninsula. Nevertheless, the old northern princes took the chance to re-establish a form of local independence, setting up on their own with Chiang Mai as their capital.

Burma became a more serious threat to Ayutthaya in the sixteenth century when its princes, who had previously been preoccupied warring among themselves, united and invaded Thailand. Their attacks reached a peak when, in 1569, they surrounded Ayutthaya, beseiged it, and finally totally laid it waste.

The future King Naresuan, the Black Prince, now appears on the scene. Captured as a child during the sacking of Ayutthaya, he was taken to Burma and, following the aristocratic code of those days, not imprisoned or executed but educated alongside the Burmese princes. Little did the Burmese know the force they were nourishing. When later they sent him back to Thailand to help with the struggle in the east against the Cambodians, the boy's success was so great that the Thais made him king at the age of sixteen.

Stucco frieze from Sukhothai, the first Thai capital and now an architectural site of world importance. Buddhism arrived in Thailand from Sri Lanka during this period.

Naresuan had, in the process of fighting his eastern neighbors, built up a huge Thai army, so large that the Burmese again perceived Ayutthaya as a threat, and so once again invaded, in 1581. Despite attacks at his rear by the Cambodians, who always took the opportunity of invading Thailand when the Thais were occupied fighting the Burmese, the young king repelled his former fellow-students, and then slew the heir apparent to the Burmese throne in a one-to-one duel. It's a story known to every Thai school-child.

King Naresuan then went on to defeat the Cambodians, punishing their earlier opportunism by having their king beheaded in public, an act the Cambodians have to this day not forgotten. Having thus defeated his two powerful neighbors, he turned on his own independently-minded brothers to the north and suppressed the Kingdom of Chiang Mai.

Naresuan the Great never succeeded in destroying the Burmese capital of Pegu, but by the end of the sixteenth century Ayutthaya was once again the dominant force in the region. He died in 1605.

EARLY EUROPEAN INFLUENCES

The initial Thai contact with a European power occurred in 1518. The Portuguese had seized Malacca in 1511, and the Thais concluded a treaty with the newcomers granting them open access to the country. They also permitted them to set up a Catholic mission in Ayutthaya, and the king even donated money towards the construction of a church there.

The other European nations who followed in the footsteps of the Portuguese were at first treated with equal generosity. A treaty was concluded with the Dutch in the early sixteenth century, and then with the British shortly afterwards.

It wasn't long, however, before the Dutch saw fit to use strong arm methods

Seated Buddha from Wat Mahathat, Sukhothai. Large Buddhas, similarly adorned with a yellow cloth, can be seen all over Thailand.

to secure the details of their demands. They quickly became so threatening that when King Nerai succeeded to the Thai throne in 1657 he took stern measures to limit Dutch influence in the country.

The Thais had already begun to react against foreign attempts to control them when in 1632 they massacred a number of Japanese who had been trying to influence court politics. In fact King Nerai's moves against the Dutch began what was to be a long Thai tradition of playing off one European power against another.

But his attempt to persuade the British East India Company to agree to assist him in the event of further Dutch tricks failed, so Nerai turned to the French who had by now also appeared on the scene. In 1664 the Thais permitted French missionaries to establish themselves in Ayutthaya, and there was even talk of a formal alliance between Louis XIV and the Thai king.

The Thai belief, however, that some benefit could be derived one way or another from these meddlesome newcomers was short-lived. Events came to a head with the arrival of a Greek adventurer named Constantine Paulkon, originally an official with the British East India Company. Paulkon began by working in an advisory capacity with the Thai government, but soon gained the king's confidence to such an extent that he was made Minister in charge of Trade, and then Chief Minister.

Naturally the highly placed Thais were both jealous and resentful, but for the moment they had to bide their time. Paulkon was quickly instrumental in furthering the idea of a Thai-French alliance, and in 1687 six French warships carrying 636 soldiers arrived in the Thai port of Bangkok. But it wasn't long before it became clear to everyone that the French were primarily interested in converting the Thais, and especially the king, to Christianity. The disenchanted Thai nobles seized their chance when the king fell ill in 1688. They staged a coup and had Paulkon arrested and exe-

Vigor and grace – detail of a carved lintel from the twelth century Khmer settlement at Pimai.

cuted, along with a number of French missionaries, including the bishop. For all intents and purposes, this was the end of European influence in Thailand for 130 years.

DECLINE AND REVIVAL

During the eighteenth century Thailand became weak, engrossed in domestic conflicts and attacked on all sides by neighbors who saw their chance for territorial expansion. This train of events reached its climax when the Burmese, temporarily united, invaded Thailand and, in 1767, completely destroyed the glorious capital of Ayutthaya. This is seen by the Thais as their darkest hour, and the country almost ceased to exist as its provinces were either annexed by foreigners or made into personal fiefdoms by dissident members of the Thai nobility.

The Thai resurgence began with a new king, Taksin. A military man of humble birth, he had escaped from the siege of Ayutthaya with 500 men and fled east into Cambodia. There he raised and trained a new army, and the following year marched on the ruins of Ayutthaya and easily defeated the Burmese garrison. Proclaiming himself king, he established a new capital at Thonburi, the western part of modern Bangkok. In 1771 he invaded Cambodia and proclaimed it a vassal state. Thailand was back on its feet again.

Taksin, however, was doomed to be the only king of his dynasty. In 1781 he was overthrown by a palace coup and executed. One General Chakri was proclaimed king, and took the title of Rama I.

A MODERNIZING DYNASTY

Chakri had been a successful military leader during Taksin's campaigns. He had defended Chiang Mai against the Burmese and had gone on to seize the Laotian kingdoms that had their capitals in modern-day Vientiane and Luang Prabang. They remained under Thai control until 1893.

King Chakri moved his capital over the river from Thonburi to Bangkok proper,

Thailand's leading commercial center. With the colonization of Burma by the British, and the country successfully aggressive on its eastern flank, Thailand's position appeared relatively secure.

The nineteenth century, however, saw Thailand under its new dynasty beginning to defend itself against the fast-expanding colonial powers on its borders.

To the south, the British were extending their control in the Malay States. In 1826 Rama III signed a treaty with them recognizing their rights in Penang while in return securing Thai trading rights elsewhere in the area. And up to the death of Rama III in 1851, British, and later American, attempts to conclude treaties giving them more extensive trading rights in Thailand were successfully resisted.

KING MONGKUT

Rama IV, King Mongkut, is one of the great Thai monarchs. He had learnt to speak and write English from American missionaries, and in addition had an enquiring mind that was fascinated by the scientific and technological developments in the West in the mid-nineteenth century. Rama III had been his brother, and had seized power on the death of their father despite Mongkut's stronger claim. Mongkut spent his long wait for the kingship as a priest and had plenty of time to develop his mind free from the worry of affairs of state.

It wasn't merely that Mongkut had had a Western education and was well versed in Western ideas. He also had the sobering experience of seeing the British defeat the Chinese Empire in the Opium War of 1841–2, the war which led to the ceding of Hong Kong to the British. If China, Thailand's greatest patron over the centuries, could not resist the Europeans with their iron ships, what hope of success did the relatively powerless Thais have?

Consequently, four years after his accession, Mongkut concluded a Treaty of Friendship and Commerce (known as the Bowring Treaty of 1855) with the British.

This allowed opium, which the British were growing in India and selling in China, more or less free access into the country, fixed the Thai duty on English goods at a mere pittance, and allowed the British exemption from Thai laws while resident in Thailand. Similar treaties were concluded with the United States and other nations, culminating, in 1898, with one with Japan.

THE FRENCH THREAT

Meanwhile, to the east, the French were establishing themselves in the southern part of Vietnam, and laying claim to Cambodia. Following a long period of pressure, Mongkut finally concluded a treaty with them in 1867 relinquishing his claim to exercise what amounted to control over most of Cambodia.

Mongkut's son, Chulalongkorn, succeeded to the throne on his father's death in 1868 and reigned until 1910. A boy on his accession, he assumed full power in 1873.

Under Chulalongkorn, Rama V, Westernization was speeded up. The royal family were obliged to learn English, and many of the king's own sons were sent to Europe to be educated.

During the 1880s, the French extended their authority into Cambodia, and then into parts of Laos where they challenged the Thai position in the rest of the country. In 1893 France demanded that Thailand abandon its claim to all territory east of the Mekong. The Thais appealed to the British for help, but the British were reluctant to become involved with the French in Asia and counseled a policy of "moderation", one that would have doomed the Thais to defeat and eventual colonization.

What became known as the Paknam Incident occurred that July. The French sent warships up the Chao Phraya River and the Thai fortress at Paknam fired on them. The French fired back, but lost no time in sending the Thais a list of demands, including extensive territorial ones, as reparation for Thai "aggression". The British refused to do more than put in a token appearance on behalf of the Thais, and in October a treaty was signed agreeing to all the French demands.

Yet in a sense Thailand benefited from the presence of two powerful European nations in the area, for in 1896 Britain and France agreed to the continuing independence of Thailand, though stripped of its former garrisons in Laos. The matter was tied up in the early years of this century when Thai independence was again confirmed but at the expense of the surrender of four states in the north of modern-day Malaysia — Kelantan, Trengganu, Kedah and Perlis — to the British, and all of modern-day Laos to the French.

THE TWENTIETH CENTURY

At the beginning of this century, Thailand and Japan were the only truly independent states in the Far East. Both were traditional monarchies who had sought to modernize and develop their contacts with the West. But whereas Japan remained independent through its military power (it defeated the Russians in a war in 1904), Thailand probably remained independent through a combination of luck and the willingness of the British to allow the French to take territory in the east in exchange for the consolidation of a superior British trading position in an independent, though territorially reduced, Thailand.

By the time World War One broke out in Europe, Rama VI (King Wachirawut, 1910–25) was on the throne. A lover of the arts, he declared Thailand's neutrality, but opted for the Allies when the Americans joined the conflict in 1917. Twelve hundred Thais fought in France in the last months of the war.

Rama VI was succeeded by his brother Prajadhipok (Rama VII). In 1932 a bloodless coup toppled the monarchy, but invited the king back as a constitutional Head of State on the British and Scandinavian pattern. The Democracy Monument in Bangkok celebrates this event.

Rama VIII (King Ananda Mahidol) succeeded his uncle in 1935, and one of the coup

leaders, Phibul Songkhram, emerged as head of the government later in the decade. He was destined to be around for some time.

When the Japanese embarked on their sweep through Asia after their attack on Pearl Harbor in 1941, Phibul, seeing that Malaya and Burma were bound to fall, allowed the Japanese into Thailand, but resistance to them was so strong he was forced to resign (in 1944).

In 1945 Britain and France demanded damaging penalties, including reparations,

from the Thais for siding with the Japanese, but the Americans did not join in this demand and instead mediated on behalf of the Thais with the Europeans. This led directly to increased US influence in the country, and eventually to the establishment of American bases in the 1960s.

KING BHUMIPOL

In 1946, Rama VIII was assassinated in the palace in circumstances that have never been satisfactorily explained. His brother Bhumipol, who succeeded him at the age of 19 as Rama IX, has proved immensely popular, and is seen by the overwhelming majority of Thais as father of the people and a man dedicated to the welfare of his subjects.

King Bhumipol's reign has, however, not been without its problems. The ideals

Buddha image regarding a *chedi* at Kampong Phet, momuments that once would have been coated in glitteringly splendid mosaics.

of constitutionalism and democracy were quickly replaced in practice by variously defined versions of military rule. On October 14, 1973, four hundred thousand people massed at the Democracy Monument in Bangkok to demand a return to constitutional rule — as a result over a hundred were killed by riot police. The crisis was defused by the king in person when he asked the government leaders to resign and leave the country. This they did, demonstrating the extraordinary power the monarchy once again wields in contemporary Thailand.

However, on October 6, 1976 another military group, styled the National Administrative Reform Council, seized power and instituted martial law. Later coups and coup attempts followed, but in recent years it has been significant that these have failed when it has become apparent that royal support was not forthcoming.

Recently, things have greatly changed for the better. Power resides with the king, the military, and an elected assembly, with no one of them holding, in practice, absolute and unchallenged authority. It's certainly not democracy, but it isn't quite autocracy either.

Bhumipol's role in this achievement has been quite crucial. His decisive responses to coups and attempted coups, and his consistent support for moderate policies, have played a vital part in fostering Thailand's stability and economic growth in recent years.

And Thailand is certainly prospering. In the late eighties it showed one of the fastest growth rates in Asia. Foreign investment is rising fast, and tourism flourishing. These are developments that reflect stable conditions, but they are, too, ones that are bound to encourage social reform and development. It is generally stagnant or declining societies that become easy victims to tyranny, whereas prosperity leads to demands for rights to accord with new-found wealth. These demands, coming from the middle classes, have elsewhere turned out to be particularly difficult to resist.

THE MANY FACES OF BUDDHISM

A LAND OF TEMPLES

Evidence of the religion followed by all but seven percent of Thais lies on every hand. Glitteringly ornate temples adorn even the drabbest of cities, and often apparently uninhabited parts of the countryside. Saffron-robed monks are everywhere, on the trains, the buses, or just browsing through city stalls looking over the latest pop cassettes.

And Thai temples are astonishingly colorful and ornate. There is no hint of subtlety, of mellow tints and suggestive shade, as in northern Europe. A brilliance and energy that rises up to greet the sun is the Thai way. Somerset Maugham thought they were "like prizes in a shooting-gallery at a village fair in the country of the gods."

There are around a quarter of a million monks in Thailand. Traditionally, all Thai men enter a monastery for three months at around the age of twenty. Some spend a shorter time there, but many go much earlier, and for several years. Some enter monasteries as a means of supporting themselves while they receive an education elsewhere, others to gain merit for their parents.

Gaining merit is central to Thai Buddhism. It's a way of storing up virtue for the next life and can be done by giving money or food to monks or to the poor as well as by entering monasteries.

Buddhism is not so much a religion as a system of philosophy. Certainly the Buddha is not understood as a god, at least in the Theravada school that Thailand follows, but as a teacher. Monks are people who, for short periods or for their whole lives, enter monasteries to study Buddhist teachings and practise the disciplines that lead to successful renunciation of the world.

Popular veneration of the monarch – dried flowers adorning the picture of King Bhumipol on a float in a festival parade in a Bangkok street.

THE LIGHT OF ASIA

Buddhism came to Thailand from Sri Lanka during the Sukhothai period.

The Lord Buddha was born Siddhartha Gautama, son of a local prince, between 563 and 556 BC in what is now Nepal. Living at first in luxury, he had married and fathered a son before, at the age of 29, he left the palace and witnessed the suffering in the outside world. After much searching for the meaning of this suffering, he sat down under a *bo* tree at Uruvela, near Gaya in Bihar State, India, and achieved "enlightenment".

Gautama's answer to the problem of suffering was contained in the Four Noble Truths, that all existence involves suffering, that this suffering is caused by desire, that in order to remove suffering you must escape desire, and that the way to escape desire is to follow the Eight-fold Path. This path details the ways to become disentangled from all desire for worldly gratification.

At Benares (Varanasi) Gautama met five Brahmins who became his first disciples. Called "the Buddha", or the Enlightened One, Gautama reputedly died aged eighty after having eaten poisoned food.

Buddhism at first flourished in India, but later died out as the older Hinduism reasserted itself. Now it is found mainly in the countries to the east, north and south of the sub-continent, in Burma, Thailand, Laos, Cambodia, Vietnam, Tibet, Nepal, China, Korea, Japan and Sri Lanka. There are virtually no Buddhists in modern India.

In the third century BC Buddhism split. Thailand follows the Theravada, or "lesser vehicle" form, so-called because it retains only the simple elements of the religion, whereas the Mahayana school, the "greater vehicle", contains many later accretions.

The half-buried Buddha image in Wat Phra Thong, Phuket. The image was discovered in this state and the temple erected over it.

THE LANGUAGE OF THE TEMPLES

It's useful to understand a few terms in connection with the architectural features of Thai temples.

The *boht* is the room housing the principal Buddha, a rectangular hall with elaborately painted doors and shutters surrounded by eight boundary stones. Its roof is usually decorated with a horn-shaped curl, or *chofa*, at each corner.

be seen in court ritual and marriage ceremonies. What interest, after all, has Buddhism, a religion of renunciation, in sanctifying as natural a state as marriage? Many of the great Thai festivals, too, such as Songkran and the Ploughing Ceremony, are Brahminic in origin.

Homes for Ghosts

Similarly, the ubiquitous spirit houses seen everywhere in the country are residues from an older set of beliefs. These brightly-

The *viharn* is a space used for assemblies of non-monks. A *chedi* is a tall structure shaped rather like a hand-bell and usually painted white. Called in India a "stupa", it generally houses a valuable relic or the ashes of an eminent (and devout) person. The *ho rakang* is a tower with a bell, or drum, at the top.

OTHER ESSENCES

Brahminism

In addition to Buddhism, elements of Brahminism, adopted by the earliest Thai kings from the Khmers and itself also of Indian origin, are still evident in Thai life. It can

painted little structures standing on the top of posts in the grounds of houses are intended to attract the spirits that might otherwise inhabit the house itself. Little plaster figures stand around representing what the spirits will be rewarded with if they resist the temptation to molest the human inhabitants of the real house. Fruit and incense sticks are also often added.

THE MOSLEM SOUTH

There are some Catholics in Thailand, but the most visible minority religion is Islam.

Thailand's Moslems are almost all in the south, close to the border with Islamic

Malaysia. Here mosques replace temples, and the call of the muezzin punctuates small town life. Not surprisingly, it's here at Pattani, in Yala Province, that Thailand's biggest mosque is to be found.

HOW THEY LIVE

LIFE ON A DOLLAR A DAY

Bangkok's teeming traffic, the gorgeous

average citizen of the USA earns seventeen times more in a year than the average Thai.

It's not a bad introduction to the fundamental realities of the country to ask one of the waiters in your hotel how much he's earning. Thais as a rule don't mind in the slightest giving this kind of information.

What you'll find is that in the average tourist-oriented restaurant on Phuket or Koh Samui he'll be earning around 30 baht (a little over one US dollar) a day, and

beaches of the islands, the deserted sandy roads between wooded hills in the north, the transvestite dancers, the itinerant street-sellers, the crowded buses, the monks — Thailand can at first precipitate considerable culture shock. What, then, lies behind all this diversity and profusion? What makes these people tick?

You only have to walk down the sois numbered in the twenties and thirties off Bangkok's Sukhumvit Road and see the armed guards and walled enclosures of the rich, and then take a look at one of the many slums (such as Klong Toey) to know you are no longer in Europe, Japan or North America. It's worth remembering that the

working a seven-day week with two free days a month — just time enough to visit his family, possibly several hundred miles away. He will sleep on the premises in a room shared with several others, and receive one or two meals a day of rice with egg and vegetables (rarely meat).

Yet, despite the fact that you'll be spending more than his daily wage on every meal you take, he will almost invariably serve it up to you cheerfully and politely, and be genuinely honored that you have chosen to take your holiday in his country.

OPPOSITE: gold-leaf being placed on a Buddha image in Nakhom Phathom; ABOVE: gold lacquer doors at Wat Phra Singh, Chiang Mai.

UPWARD MOBILITY

But this is Asia, where only a few generations ago men crawled in the presence of the monarch, and after childbirth women were roasted in front of a fire until their bodies blistered. Given the historical background of absolutism and superstition, Thailand has made remarkable progress. It can't yet match the most successful countries of Asia, but it has already lifted itself a long way out of the bottom league.

Evidence of the new and burgeoning middle class is everywhere. The highways are lined with bill-boards advertising dream houses that would look more at home in Texas than tropical Asia. And a quick look at the gleaming white Gothic apartments on Soi Suan Phlu, just down the road from Bangkok's Immigration Office, will give you some idea of the fairyland lifestyles being prepared for the country's emerging bourgeoisie.

AUTHORITARIAN WAYS

Yet old ways persist. You won't have been in the country long before you see the photographs in the daily papers of accused persons in police stations, usually standing alongside some item related to their alleged offence. Few Thais see this as a violation of the rights of accused persons. Instead, such pictures are understood as proof of the continuing successes of the police in combating crime.

The position of the military, too, in Thailand is very strong. Ordinary soldiers can behave with very un-Thai arrogance in casual encounters. All male citizens are theoretically liable to military service at 21, but the catch is that, because smaller numbers are required than are available, there's a lottery to select those who will in fact serve, and it's the poor who always seem to lose. The dire significance of this becomes clear when you consider that 41 soldiers had to have legs amputated in a Bangkok hospital after treading on landmines in the 1988 conflict with Laos over a border hill so insignificant it had no name, only a number.

The remains of Old Asia can still be seen, too, in matters of public health. You need only to look at the statistics for the incidence of leprosy, and compare them with government funding available for its treatment and prevention, to see this. It's too complex a subject to deal with in a book of this nature, but the crux is that it's a disease that strikes at the undernourished — well-fed doctors dealing with cases have never been known to contract it. The continuing incidence of leprosy in a developing country such as Thailand is an indicator that there is still some way to go on the road to genuine modernization and reform.

A BRIGHTLY LIT FUTURE

Even so, the Thais still manage to present a cheerful face to life in a way that has become legendary. In addition, perhaps *because* the classes are so sharply distinct, there is an absence of the endless attention to exact social status, and all the petty snobberies that go with this, observable in such long-democratic states as the United Kingdom. There is a charm about Thai life that travelers have been commenting on for centuries, and it still persists. And as economic growth continues, so Thailand will with luck move into the position of having the best of both worlds, the traditions and natural blessings that already make it such an attractive tourist destination and the comfort and sense of well-being that goes with a country emerging into the bright light of economic prosperity.

MONARCHISM

No visitor to the country can fail to be struck by the devotion of ordinary Thais to their king. Not only does Bumiphol's picture hang everywhere, but also the pictures of the beloved nineteenth century kings

Chulalongkorn and Mongkut. Talk to a peasant in his rice-paddy and he will refer, not to "the king" but to "'my king". Limestone caves all over the kingdom contain rocks signed with the royal initials to commemorate a visit. And there are few big festivals in Bangkok not graced by the presence of one of the royal family with guards with horse-hair plumes of every color of the rainbow in evidence.

There is an element of the veneration of the priest-kings of old in all this. The Thai

for their education. And there is no doubt whatsoever that the present ruler, King Bhumipol, stands resolutely and unambiguously in that tradition.

A MONASTIC PERSPECTIVE

Every Buddhist Thai male spends a period of his youth living in a temple, and many return for periods of varying length in later life. Given this fact, a visit to, and preferably a few days' residence in, a Thai temple can

royal family leans heavily for its legitimization on Buddhism — or rather Brahminism: pure Buddhism has no concern for affairs of state. The way the king is regarded by the average Thai is close to worship, and contains in almost all cases no element of envy or resentment. (It should be said, though, that the Thai monarchy is well protected by a strong *lese-majeste* law against any public criticism.)

Nevertheless, there is a tradition going back to Kings Mongkut and Chulalongkorn in the last century of the monarch being in the forefront of the drive for modernization, a tradition fostered by the custom of sending young Thai princes to Europe

add a whole new dimension to a stay in the country.

It's relatively easy for men to arrange this, considerably more difficult for women. But in either case what you should do is approach any English-speaking monk in any temple and politely ask how such a visit might be arranged.

What you will find is a way of life that begins at four in the morning with two hours of chanting and meditation, followed

ABOVE: King Bhumipol takes the salute on the King's Birthday parade outside the National Assembly building in Bangkok. Cavalry and infantry alike are decked out in brilliantly-colored plumes.

by a walk through the nearby streets begging for offerings of food.

Once breakfast is over, various tasks are undertaken, and then the main meal of the day is served shortly before noon. Thai monks, following the practice of the Lord Buddha, are not permitted to eat anything after midday.

For accommodation you'll be provided with a wooden palette and a thin cloth. If you're lucky, you might get a bottle of Coca Cola with which to fight off

the pangs of hunger during the long hot night.

Most people, though, will be content to visit a typical monastery rather more briefly. The big Bangkok temples are not the best choice — there are so many tourists in evidence the monks tend, not surprisingly, to be on the defensive. Choose, instead, somewhere up-country, or one of the Bangkok temples not mentioned in this, or any, guide-book. You'll soon know if you've hit on a suitable place — if you're welcome, it'll be the monks themselves who will smile first, and if you smile back, quickly approach you and begin to try out their English.

A New Direction

If, however, you're not only seriously interested in Buddhism but also eager to experience its purer manifestations, you

Thai monks — ABOVE: on the pre-breakfast begging round; OPPOSITE: a tattooed monk prays in Wat Maharat, Sukhothai.

could do a lot worse than visit Bangkok's Wat Santiasoke where a radical abbot, Phra Pottilux, is leading his community along new paths. Situated in the untouristed Bundkapi district, it isn't easy to find. But it's a place that has seen many eminent Thais, from Bangkok's Governor Chamlong downwards, arrive to pay homage.

When I went there it was a Sunday, and most of the laymen there were dressed in the traditional plain blue smocks of the rural poor. My guide took his rings off. "Too much fashion," he said. "It isn't proper."

Everything at Wat Santiasoke is reasonable and thought-out. Sunday has been adopted as a "venerable day" because that fits in with the international week/weekend routine, and temple rituals are conducted in Thai whenever possible. When the traditional Pali is used (a dead Indian language few Thais understand), there is simultaneous translation into Thai.

The temple has revived vegetarianism, an ancient Buddhist principle, even though Thai Buddhism does not formally adhere to it. The approach road is lined with vegetarian food stalls, and round the corner on the main road there are food shops so dedicated to service rather than profit that they display the prices they pay for items in brackets alongside the prices they charge the customer.

Inside the temple compound, monks sat laughing and talking to lay people about their problems. There were all classes of people there, the guide said, millionaires and farmers, doctors and factory workers. Someone was getting a very close "student" haircut — "clean and cool, but also indicating austerity" — and other people were laying out herbs to dry in the sun.

Some monks were involved in making copies of cassettes of the Phra Pottilux's sermons, to be loaned out free of charge, while others were setting up type for printed versions. Generally the atmosphere was one of ordered, varied and meaningful work.

Wat Santiasoke is a sign of new directions in Thai Buddhism. I asked to see the main sanctuary and was shown a plain hall that bore no relation to the gaudily painted *boht* of a regular temple.

"We don't waste time on that sort of thing here," said the guide.

MASSAGE FOR MALES

All the world knows, however, that the Thais are not solely a devout and self-

denying people. Bangkok's massage parlours are celebrated the world over, and the curious male tourist won't take long to discover that they're not confined to the capital. The first-time visitor might be surprised, however, to learn that the phenomenon is not a product of foreign tourism, or of the American troop presence during the Vietnam War. Ranks of girls sitting behind a glass window with numbers round their necks can be seen in provincial hotels up and down the country, with not a foreigner in sight. For better or worse, it's a social institution that's gained a wider acceptance in Thailand than perhaps anywhere else in the world.

The reasons for this are not difficult to find. On the one hand the social, and economic, dominance of the male has a long history in Southeast Asia; on the other, Buddhism has never regarded what other religions have dubbed "the sins of the flesh" particularly seriously.

And it would be foolish to try to pretend that Thailand's reputation as a land of easy sex isn't a major ingredient in its tourist appeal. Statistics show that unaccompanied males constitute a far higher proportion of visitors here than they do in most other comparable countries.

Other than that, there's little that can be said. Some people think it's a phenomenon that sadly spoils an otherwise delightful country, others will say that the Thais involved go about their work with such ingenuous charm they are enough to give the business a good name. In a country where a man can take a "junior wife" (*mia noi*), they argue, what on earth's wrong in taking a wife just for the night. Here, rather more literally than in most other spheres, you pay your money and you take your choice.

A LIFE IN THE HILLS

By and large the Thais are a homogeneous people. Racial minorities, apart from the large Chinese presence in Bangkok and other major cities, are confined to the Malay or part-Malay Muslims in the south and the curious and much discussed hill-tribes in the north.

The mysterious arrival of these people in Thailand is the subject of much debate. A study of their languages shows many of the tribes originate in the Tibetan plateau. Most of them only migrated to Thailand this century.

What makes the hill tribes of northern Thailand so fascinating is that these largely migrant people will have no truck with city life. They remain essentially classless, continue to dress for the most part in traditional costume, are content to cultivate land the Thais don't want, and stubbornly grow and smoke opium.

The Thai government is making strenuous efforts both to improve their standard of living and to encourage them to conform to more socially acceptable life-styles. Prominent in this program is the Royal Development Project for the Hill Tribes.

There are however, considerable difficulties involved in this approach. On the one hand the opium poppy which the hill tribes are so adept at cultivating, and to which many of them are addicted, is the

There's no problem at all in actually getting to see the hill people. Trekking is one of the main tourist activities up in the north, and treks out of Chiang Mai and Chiang Rai invariably advertise a night or two in hill-tribe villages as among their key attractions.

And despite everything, the presence — so close to a modern society — of traditionally-dressed people living their lives very largely according to the dictates of their opium dreams cannot fail to con-

source of lethal heroin addiction in the cities, in Thailand and elsewhere. But on the other hand their way of life is not something that ought to be obliterated by the demands of conformity and integration under the guise of drug-control.

Furthermore, the hill tribes are a major attraction for tourists, so much so that over-exposure to foreigners is fast becoming one of the biggest threats to their traditional life-style. There's no doubt that the hill tribes' popularity with foreigners is one of the main reasons why the Thais are likely to go easy in any attempt to coerce these colorful outsiders in their midst into a more regular mode of existence.

stitute an attraction for young visitors deeply drawn to the romantic call of such an apparently carefree life-style.

A PASTORAL LIFE

The overwhelming majority of Thais still live and work in the countryside. There is, of course, considerable poverty and deprivation; nevertheless most of Thailand remains an immensely pleasant place.

Thai temples, always ornate and sometimes gorgeous, are often in addition surprising, and even on occasions odd. OPPOSITE: a rare Hindu temple, Silom Road, Bangkok; ABOVE: eyes unexpectedly regard you at Wat Yannawa, Bangkok.

Images of the traditional pastoral life, though, complete with elephants, and fishing from sailing boats, are nowadays rather wide of the mark. Elephants, anyway, were never used in farming — their original function in ancient Siam was ceremonial, and as instruments of war. White elephants were given to each other as presents by kings throughout Southeast Asia, and if one was stolen by an enemy, wars were waged to retrieve them.

When in the 1880s foreign nations won

concessions to fell and extract timber, the British came up with the idea of training elephants specifically for the job. Though today their role has largely been taken over by machines, there are still around ten thousand of them working in the teak forests of the north, or in the far south near the Malaysian border. They are used in rough jungle terrain to bring logs to the edge of forest roads where they can be collected by trucks. An adult can haul two tonnes, and lift 700 kilos with its tusks.

But the best places to see them are elsewhere. Treks in the north usually contain a two-hour ride on an elephant as part of the journey, and elephant shows feature in the displays of Thai country life put on at places like the Rose Garden outside Bangkok and Pattaya's Nong Nooch Village. There's also a daily show at Pattaya's Elephant Village, just outside the town. And the biggest show of all is the annual

Northern hill tribes — ABOVE: Akha women and children; RIGHT: Akha girls picking opium poppies.

Elephant Round-Up, organized by the Tourist Authority of Thailand (TAT) at Surin every November.

There are a hundred or so wild elephants in the Khao Yai National Park, 205 km (128 miles) north of Bangkok. This is the best place in Thailand, and one of the best in Asia for observing tropical nature, including some large animals, in its natural state. Contact TAT for full details.

In addition, the government runs a Young Elephant Training Center north of Lampang (see NORTHERN THAILAND section in THE BROAD HIGHWAY for details) where the animals are prepared for forest work, and tourists are welcome.

FISHERMEN OF THE SOUTH

Songkhla, on the Gulf of Siam, claims to be the largest fishing port in Asia, but it's on the other side of the isthmus, in the thinly populated southwest, that fishermen's life can be seen at its most relaxed. There's also more coral here than in the southeast — coral needs abundant sunlight, and the clear water of the Andaman Sea provides ideal conditions for its growth.

But even in such a natural paradise as the coast of Krabi and Trang provinces, there are problems. Reefs have been damaged or destroyed by the dynamiting for fish, and by the use of heavy anchors. And the grotesque proposal to put down old car tyres covered in cement as substitute breeding grounds for fish demonstrates just how far things have gone in some areas.

THAI PLEASURES

SING A SONG!

Traditional Thai music is a wild, energetic sound played with *pi* (a sort of oboe), *sor* and *pin* (stringed instruments), wooden xylophones as found in Indonesia, and drums. It can be difficult to get to hear,

however. You hear it, of course, at the boxing matches, and sometimes you come across it in taxis or on buses. Easiest perhaps is to ask for it at the numerous cassette stalls in Bangkok.

By contrast, the music visitors hear most of the time in Thailand is astonishingly Western. Popular music is a thriving industry and, despite its remoteness from traditional Thai music, has a very memorable and engaging local flavor.

In addition, the Thais do love to sing. What they sing are usually the current hits, and it doesn't usually take much to get them going. "Sing a song!" is a frequent cry, and it doesn't always need a bottle of Mekong whiskey to persuade the singer, though that undoubtedly helps.

Dance

Unfortunately, classical Thai dancing is not in a very healthy state. It's most easily seen in restaurants laying it on as an extra draw for tourists, or as performed by the rather tired dancers at the Erawan Shrine in Bangkok.

You might be lucky enough to catch something of better quality on your travels, though. Ask TAT or the Siam Society (see p. 67) in Bangkok for advice if this is your special interest.

THAI GAMES

Very common in Thailand is that wonderful and rare thing, a non-competitive group game. In **takraw** half a dozen young men in a circle try to keep a light ball made of braided rattan in the air by any means other than their hands. You see this game played everywhere — in courtyards, on waste ground or in parks. There are competitive forms too, though. One has teams on either side of a net, and another is very similar to basket ball. Both retain the rule forbidding touching the ball with the hands.

Rather less common is **krabi krabong**, sword fighting with two swords. This is

Setting out for the day's work in the fields north of Chiang Mai.

almost invariably nowadays put on as part of a public display by accomplished professionals.

Kite Flying

The Thais, like the Chinese, have been flying kites for at least as long as records go back. In olden times kites were used in war, carrying explosives over, and then down onto, enemy fortifications. In more recent times, the art reached its zenith as a popular sport during the reign of King Chulalong-

A NIGHT AT THE RINGSIDE

But the sport most beloved by Thais is their own national form of boxing. There are two major venues in Bangkok, and of these it's the Lumpini Stadium that has more atmosphere and gives a stronger feeling of this most Thai of sports.

The Lumpini Stadium is slightly difficult to find. Coming on foot along Rama 4 from Lumpini Park, it's immediately after

korn (Rama V) when the palace was forced to promulgate laws to curb the practice of kite flying in the capital as kites were becoming entangled on the turrets of public buildings.

Your best chance of seeing formal kite-flying contests nowadays in Bangkok is at **Senam Luang** (a grassy open space opposite the National Theatre and National Museum) during March and April. The Large "male" kites *(chula)* battle with smaller but more nimble "female" ones *(pakpao)*, each group of enthusiasts attempting to ensnare the others' kites and drag them across to enemy territory.

the Royal Thai Armed Forces Preparatory Academy, the large formal building behind railings, just by where the shops begin. It's set back a few meters from the road but is immediately recognizable by the mass of food stalls that cluster round the entrance.

The stadium itself has a corrugated iron roof, wooden seats, and barbed wire above the wire-mesh barricades separating the second and third class areas. Neon lights and fans are fixed to the roof. It's all rather rough and ready, old and well-used. There are a few simple advertisements for Coca Cola etc. Boys aged about ten walk round selling Liprovitan D, a very popular vitamin tonic, served on ice. Framed black and white photos of famous fighters hang by the entrance to the Ringside enclosure.

If you go into the third class area early, just before 6 pm, you can join the enthusiasts looking over the back row of seats at the boxers being prepared for the fights.

A Fight Remembered

The two being made ready for the first bout lie on tables, their heads on their

kit-bags, while two masseurs apiece work over them energetically using embrocation the color of orange-juice. They bind their hands tightly with white bandages, securing the ends with white masking tape.

Compared with Western boxers these all seem featherweights. One of them looks about 17. The smell of the embrocation is everywhere. A girl comes forward carrying a pair of red and yellow shorts newly emblazoned with a motto. These are now put on, preceded by a jockstrap and a guard. The assistants then secure their gloves with more white tape. Pink socks follow, tight and without toes. A rose-colored towel

is then placed over the fighter's slender shoulders, followed by a magnificent red and gold cape.

Finally, round his head goes the "mong-kun", a rigid headband with a long protruding tail. Before he puts this on, one of the two assistants blesses it by holding it momentarily to his lips. The boxer then leaves down a corridor, like a lion at a circus, and emerges moments later by the ring. He takes his place in a sort of iron pen, accompanied by one assistant.

The stadium is now beginning to fill up. A bell rings and everyone stands. The National Anthem is played.

Then a strange, wild note on the *pi* rings out from the three-piece band. The boxers go onto their knees in the middle of the ring and bow to each other. One of them then performs a dance to the music, as if getting himself into a trance. The dancers dance — and fight — barefoot.

Then the music stops again and the referee appears. There is a prayer, and the mongkuns are taken off. When the music starts again, the first round begins — with a couple of playful kicks.

The band consists of an "oboist" playing his *pi*, a drummer with a pair of long conga-type drums, and a player with a pair of high-pitched cymbals. The musicians play only during the actual fighting.

Between rounds the contestants sit on stools to be sponged down. The stool stands on a large tin tray that protects the ring and its canvas cover from the water.

By the second and third rounds the crowd is shouting. Bets are being laid everywhere, men holding up various numbers of fingers to indicate the odds. Every blow, by knee, elbow. foot or fist, is cheered with a part-approving, part sympathetic "ooo-ah".

Suddenly it's all over. There are five bouts of three minutes each in Thai boxing matches, with two minute rests between them. Now his assistant carries one of the contestants from the center of the ring, not because he can't walk but in order to hold him on high. The fighter responds by holding his arms out like a wooden Christ. Meanwhile the other fighter is given a vigorous massage. And then it's on to the next bout.

Backstage again, the assistant helps the boxer disrobe. But he takes the tape and bandages off his hands himself, tearing at them in impatience with his teeth. There is no sense of victory or defeat, merely of a short job done. No injuries whatsoever are visible. It seems that because of all the kicking and elbowing, there is less empha-

As well as the food stalls, there are also shops selling mongkuns, shorts, embrocation — anything, in fact, associated with the sport. The trade mark on almost all the items of clothing is the same — "Windy".

FESTIVALS

Asian festivals are something very special. They have a vigor and a reality about them that has disappeared from festivals in the

sis on actual punches, and as a result less physical injury than in the Western version.

After their work, the assistants backstage look at magazines featuring photos of boxers and of recent bouts. The contestant, now dressed in T-shirt and jeans, with his kit in a bag slung over his shoulder, leaves as casually as a student off for a jog in Lumpini Park.

Outside the food stalls are doing a brisk business as more people arrive for the bigger fights. There are six per night, with the fifth traditionally involving the most celebrated fighters. The young contestant of the first bout takes a bowl of soup at one of the stalls.

West, with the exception of Christmas. With their colorful outdoor processions, their huge crowds and the general air of something that is at one and the same time great fun and of profound significance, Thai festivals can hold their own with any in the region.

For the poor especially, they are events that help compensate for the restricted opportunities of life, and they also serve to bind the whole of society together in a

Thai games – OPPOSITE: kites in the April sky; ABOVE: contestants pay their respects to their patrons before a bout of Thai boxing at Bangkok's Rose Garden.

way that members of more materialistically advanced cultures, Western and Eastern, may envy.

Because the dates of most festivals are calculated according to a lunar calendar, their dates on the international, Western calendar, which is based on the sun, vary from year to year. Only Songkran, the annual New Year ceremony, together with certain modern anniversaries such as Chakri Day and the royal birthdays, occur on fixed dates on the Western calendar.

COOL SEASON (NOVEMBER TO FEBRUARY)

Surin Elephant Round-up. Not really a festival, this tourist-oriented but spectacular event takes place on the third weekend of November in the northeastern town of Surin, 454 km (281 miles) from Bangkok.

Loi Krathong, "floating the leaf-cup". This is the time when Thais everywhere

Long Live the King! ABOVE: the royal throne, Bangkok; OPPOSITE: Prince Vijiralongkorn, the Thai Crown Prince, pauses to accept a charitable donation from a member of the public during his father's sixtieth birthday celebrations.

make little boats and send them off on the canals containing a candle, a flower, an incense stick and a coin. It falls at full moon on the twelfth lunar month. It's one of the big festivals of the Thai year, a joyful occasion marking the official end of the rainy season, and it's celebrated all over the country.

His Majesty The King's Birthday. December 5 and a national holiday. A large military parade is held in Bangkok two days before when the Royal Guards renew their allegiance to the king.

Constitution Day. This celebrates the signing of the first Thai constitution on December 10, 1932.

Chiang Mai Flower Festival. Featuring floral floats and parades, this festival — designed for tourist's cameras — takes place on the first Friday in February (only in Chiang Mai).

Magha Puja is celebrated in February or early March, on the full moon of the third lunar month. It's essentially a religious festival, with sermons, offerings to monks, and freeing of captive birds. In the evening monks and people carry candles, flowers and incense in procession three times round the temples. The festival commemorates major events in the Buddha's life and is celebrated throughout Thailand.

HOT SEASON (MARCH TO MAY)

Chakri Day is April 6. This is a national holiday to commemorate the founding of the Chakri (the present) royal dynasty.

Songkran begins on April 13 and lasts three days. Songkran is one of the great Thai festivals, celebrated throughout the country, and memorial services dedicated to departed ancestors are held. It's the traditional New Year and apart from the general hilarity, popular entertainments and a traditional skittles game called "*saba*", it involves the throwing of water as a sign of

purification. It's quite possible to step off a bus in Bangkok in all innocence and have a large bucket of water emptied over you by total strangers. Fortunately, April is the hottest month of the Thai year.

Ploughing Ceremony. This takes place in late April or early May to mark the beginning of the rice-planting season. In Bangkok, the king presides in person over the elaborate ceremonies, usually held at the open space called Senam Luang.

is at the full moon of the eighth lunar month. It marks the beginning of Thai monks' three-month retreat (called Khao Phansa) during the rainy season and commemorates the Lord Buddha's first sermon to his disciples. Devotees go to the temples with offerings for the monks confronting a long spell without contact with the rest of the world.

Queen's Birthday. August 12, and a national holiday.

Coronation Day. May 5. This commemorates King Bhumipol's coronation in 1950.

Visakha Puja. Usually in May, this most important of all Buddhist festivals takes place at the full moon on the sixth lunar month. It marks the birth, enlightenment and death of the Lord Buddha. Thais crowd into the temples and take part in candlelit processions.

Bun Bang Fai is the time in May when phallic rockets are let off in the northeast (only) in an attempt to guarantee a plentiful rice crop.

RAINY SEASON (JUNE TO OCTOBER)
Asalha Puja. Usually in July, this festival

Phuket Chinese Vegetarian Festival. Late September or early October. See under PHUKET AND THE EAST COAST for a description of this spectacular orgy of skewered cheeks, pierced tongues, ladders of knives and walking on fire.

Ok Phansa is the end of the period of retreat during the rains and usually falls in October. The period is celebrated all over

Elephants at the annual Elephant Round-up at Surin, a cross between a carnival and a rodeo in which the elephants "play football", march to music and engage in a test of strength with a team of locals via a tug-of-war — the outcome of which is never in doubt, of course.

the country with boat races wherever there is a suitable stretch of water.

Chulalongkorn Day. October 23, and a national holiday in honor of Thailand's much loved nineteenth century monarch.

FOOD AND DRINK

A Culinary Adventure

Many people talk about Thai food as if it's as likely as not to burn the skin off your tongue at the first taste. This is very far from the truth, and although some dishes can indeed be extremely spicy, the cuisine in general is pungent, fragrant and usually made with the freshest ingredients. It's an adventure that shouldn't be missed simply because of some exaggeratedly lurid travelers' tales.

Essentially, Thai food is distinctive and exciting, another experience again from the better-known Indian and Chinese cuisines that flank it to west and north. It is true that these great neighbouring civilizations have produced elaborate traditions in eating which the Thais can't in all honesty compete with. Nevertheless, with its simple country flavors, its fresh ingredients and the memorable tastes of its own distinctive herbs and spices, Thai food is a world of its own and an indispensable part of any stay, however short, in the country.

Traditional Thai food as eaten in the home is relatively uncomplicated, compared, for example, with European or Chinese. Rice and vegetables, plus some dried fish (rarely meat), together with a soup and several sauces, add up to a small banquet for the average Thai. And the same thing can be eaten at any time of day. Large restaurants, on the other hand, manage to conjure up specialities as elaborate as any on offer elsewhere in the region.

The basic ingredients of the cuisine are the natural products of the country. The Thais have always been self-sufficient in food produce, and only recently has the population explosion led to local shortages. Thailand produces a huge amount of rice, an abundance of vegetables, and, in its rivers and canals as well as off its coasts, as much fish as its people can eat. The country still manages to export large amounts of foodstuffs.

The ingredients tend to be simply and quickly cooked in a *wok*, Chinese-fashion. The spiced sauces taken with them, though, are hot and sharp in a way not often found in Chinese cooking.

As it's these sauces that are most characteristic of Thai food, it's wise to learn their names first. *Nam* is the Thai word for "water". From this follows *nam prik*, " the very hot chili sauce; *nam pla*, fish sauce, made with salted and fermented fish (anyone passing on their way to Koh Samet through Rayong, the port where much Thai *nam pla* is made, will know what it smells like); *nam man*, oil; *nam man oy*, oyster sauce; *nam manao*, lemon juice; *nam som*, vinegar; and *nam oy*, sugar-cane juice. These are usually served mixed with chopped shallots, lemon grass (a very distinctive Thai flavor), chilies, garlic or tamarind.

Finally, soy sauce is *nam si yu*, sticky rice is *khao niaw*, and the short lengths of bamboo you see people buying contain baked rice and are called *putto*.

Dishes You Might Like to Try

TOM YAM — a soup, made sharp and hot with lemon grass and chilies;
TOM YAM KUNG — as above, with prawns;
KAENG JUED — a mild-flavored soup, Chinese-style;
KHAO TOM — a clear white soup;
PLA THORD RAD KHING — fried fish with ginger;
KAENG SOM — sweet sour fish curry;
PLA NUENG JAEW MAKHUA TET — steamed fish with spicy tomato sauce;
PLA THORD PAK THAI — fried fish with garlic and ginger;
LARP NUA — spicy minced meat with mint;
MOU WAN — caramel pork;
KAENG KHIAW WAN KAI — coconut chicken curry;
POD LON — five-flavor duck;

PHAD MAKHUA SAI THUA KHIEW — aubergine with lentils;
KHAI JIEW MANGSAWIRAT — vegetable omelette;
SOM TAM MALAKOR — papaya salad;
YAM HED — mushroom salad.

Dishes for Vegetarians

Vegetarians should be able to find food to suit them even in ordinary restaurants. All the following dishes come without meat:

major tourist centers — Chiang Mai, Phuket, Koh Samui — many restaurants have sprung up run by permanent or semi-permanent foreign residents with the result that these places offer a very wide range of food indeed. In Bangkok you can eat virtually any style you can think of, but even in places like Koh Samui, Mexican, Italian, and German food can be found. German restaurants are actually particularly common in many places in Thailand.

MASAMAN MANGSAWIRAT — vegetable curry;
PHAD PHAK PRIEW WAN — sweet sour vegetables;
LARB THUA DEANG — kidney-bean salad;
KHAO PHAD THUA SAI KHAI — fried rice with beans and egg;
KHAO PHAD MANGSAWIRAT — vegetable fried rice;
TOM YAM HED MANGSAWIRAT — vegetable and mushroom soup.

The Taste of Home

Western food is on offer in all places where Westerners have ever, even briefly, put in an appearance. In Bangkok and the other

Western food varies considerably, however, in its relation to the thing back home. The ubiquitous American Breakfast, for instance, will usually see you served with two fried eggs, some bacon, cold ham or a sausage, accompanied by lettuce, tomato and cucumber, plus two slices of sweet rice bread, a pat of the world's worst margarine, and some very sweet and chemically flavored pineapple and orange marmalade. Your coffee will be instant, with non-dairy creamer; condensed milk, sweet or unsweetened, will be substituted on demand.

Fruit and Drinks

As for fruit, you'll see it all on display in

any market. Don't just stick to the kinds you know — this could prove expensive. Apples, for instance, retail at getting on for one US dollar *each* as they have to be flown in from such distant sources as New Zealand or North California. Try instead custard apples, luscious mangosteens, fragrantly delicious rambutans, sweet and sticky mangoes, or even the foul-smelling (but fine-tasting) durian.

Thais drink a lot of soft drinks, and you are certain to want to as well. But why not

For the rest, ice does these days seem to be relatively safe, though different people will have different tolerance levels. It is, though, very hard to avoid. Generally speaking, avoiding crushed ice, and taking a chance with cubes, is a reasonable strategy.

Beer is good, though expensive. Kloster is the best, closely followed by the more strongly flavored Singah. Thai whiskey, Mekong, is very cheap and excellent value for the price. You'll frequently see rows

try the fresh local varieties, squeezed citrus drinks, for instance, or, best of all, the deliciously fragrant water of the young coconut, prepared with a chopper before your eyes and served up with a straw for, in the country, as little as five baht?

Tap water is NOT drinkable anywhere in Thailand. Nor is it enough simply to boil it — in Bangkok you have to boil it for *half an hour* before considering taking it into your system, and even then the chlorine will not have been removed, just the content proportionally increased. Far better to buy the inexpensive bottled water marketed under the trade-name Polaris.

of Mekong bottles standing on shelves behind bars, each with a strip of paper stuck to it. These bottles belong to customers who have bought a bottle from the bar and have left it only partly drunk to be finished off another time. There's no reason at all why you shouldn't do the same. Sometimes the Thais drink their Mekong along with a vitamin tonic such as Liprovitan B, but it's usually — and best — drunk with Pepsi or Coca Cola.

Coconuts start their journey down river to market ABOVE and OPPOSITE, chillies. Both are dominant in Thai cuisine.

SHOPPING

Thailand is a wonderful place for shopping because it has just attained that magical point in its development where prices are still low but quality is good. There are, it's true, a lot of goods on sale manufactured specially for tourists and of no great interest. But even discounting these, there's no shortage of excellent things to buy if you know what you're looking

for — and sometimes, even if you don't.

Thai silk is available everywhere. For top quality, go to Jim Thompson's Shop in Bangkok; for lengths of rough country silk, go almost anywhere. The silk factories just outside Chiang Mai are a good place to inspect the manufacturing process and buy some of the products on the spot.

Thai tailors will run you up a suit or a dress in around twenty-four hours. Try the top end of Bangkok's Sukhumvit Road (near the Regal Landmark Hotel) for many Indian-run establishments.

Thailand is celebrated for its gems and its gold. Great caution is needed, however, if you intend to assay this market. Bargains can be had, but it's rather more likely *you* will be had if you aren't very well informed in the trade. Even so, it is possible to make sound purchases in this field if you insist the retailer comes along with you to an independent assayer for large purchases, and if you have your purchases itemised in detail on your receipt, with gold quality and weight (for example) entered in full, and 'subject to identification and appraisal by a registered gemologist' entered and signed for expensive purchases of gems.

Clothes are very cheap in Thailand — cotton shirts, for example, of quite reasonable quality can be bought for around US$4. The places to look for these are the stalls of the street vendors in Silom and Sukhumvit Roads.

In addition, craft items that can best be bought locally include Hill Tribe shoulder bags, wood-carvings and wicker-work in Chiang Mai, silverware — also in Chiang Mai — and ceramics, this last all over the northern region.

Finally, you can come across attractive and unusual small folk objects almost anywhere. Their attraction is that you'd never have conceived of their existence before you saw them — just keep your eyes open, especially in out-of-the-way places.

ABOVE: Fresh prawns, charcoal-grilled and sold as an appetising beachside snack in Pattaya. OPPOSITE: Buddha images are a part of everyone's life in Thailand. Here a selection stands on sale in a Bangkok Store.

Bangkok
and
Ayutthaya

Capitals
New and Old

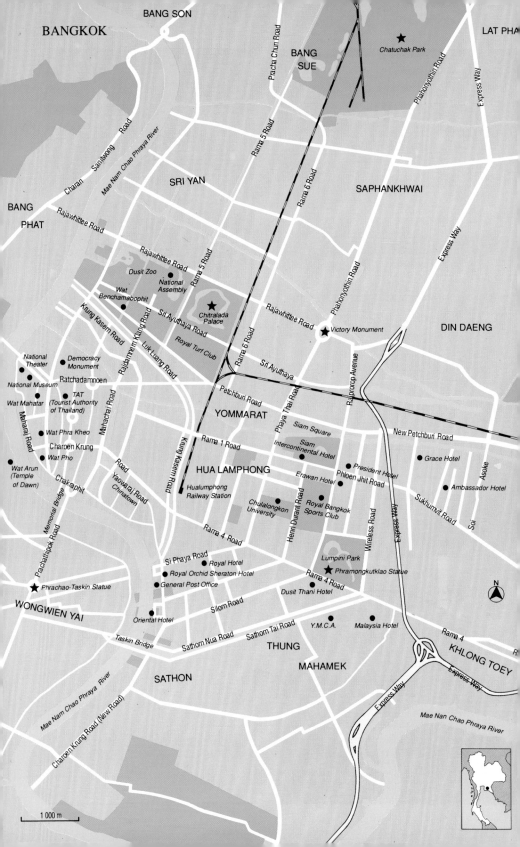

BANGKOK – ANGELIC CITY?

"It is impossible to consider these populous modern cities of the East," wrote Somerset Maugham in 1930, contemplating Bangkok, "without a certain malaise. They are all alike, with their straight streets, their arcades, their tramways, their dust, their blinding sun, their teeming Chinese, their dense traffic, their ceaseless din. They have no history, no traditions. Painters have not painted them. No poets, transfiguring dead bricks and mortar with their divine nostalgia, have given them a tremulous melancholy not their own. They live their own lives, without associations, like a man without imagination...They give you nothing. But when you leave them it is with a feeling that you have missed something, and you cannot help thinking that they had some secret that they have kept from you. And although you have been a trifle bored, you look back upon them wistfully; you are certain they have after all something to give you which, had you stayed longer, or under other conditions, you would have been capable of receiving."

Bangkok ("town of olives", more often called by the Thais "Krung Thep", "city of angels") no longer has trams, and the Chinese teem no more than anybody else. Few people, either, are these days bored in Bangkok. But the city nevertheless remains on first acquaintance a slightly forbidding place.

Other cities have their compensations, features such as surrounding mountains, a frontage on the sea, or an inheritance of spacious public parks, that help in some measure at least to counteract the horrors of the modern megalopolis. Bangkok has none of these. Instead, under torrid tropical skies, and with no underground or suburban railway system, it seems a city permanently held to ransom by its traffic.

Nevertheless, Bangkok is crammed with attractions. Like any capital, it exudes interest simply by virtue of the fact that it draws to it so much of the country's vital life. Its nightlife is famous — notorious if you will — all over the world. Its temples, crowded though they may be with visitors, are anything but the lethargically picturesque structures that add such interest to the rest of the countryside. Bangkok was made into the Thai capital, almost by an act of will, in the early nineteenth century, and for better or worse it now exhibits all the features you'd expect from the metropolis of one of Asia's most fast-developing nations.

In addition, as the centre of government and home base of the Thai royal family, Bangkok periodically lays on parades and ritual ceremonies more splendid — and photogenic — than can be found anywhere else in the country. To watch the parade of the royal guards outside the National Assembly building on one of the royal anniversaries is to see as colorful a mix of Western and Asian, ancient and

Thai serenity and languor? An Italian statue, carved in the Carrara marble Michaelangelo used, imported from Europe by nineteenth century King Mongkut (Rama IV). The royal summer residence at Bang Pa-In — no longer used and now open to the public; see p.79.

modern, as you can witness anywhere in the region.

And as for a modicum of peace and quiet, the Chao Phraya River does provide something of a respite from the noise, and even from the heat, of this tumultuous and at times oppressive conurbation.

Even so, it's as well for first-time visitors to come prepared. Bangkok does have its attractions, and they are real ones, but the transport problem is such that they do nowadays come dangerously close to being eclipsed by the mechanical onslaught.

We suggest that a short time spent studying the following two sections, and referring to the maps on pages 50, will acquaint you with the main areas and lines of communication of the city, and stand you in good stead for coming to terms with the sometimes difficult situation on the ground.

A BIRD'S EYE VIEW

Bangkok mostly lies to the east of two bends in the Chao Phraya River.

West of the river is Thonburi, an extensive area but one that contains only one notable monument, Wat Arun (Temple of the Dawn).The modern center of Bangkok is all on the eastern side.

The Historic Center

Close to the river, and directly opposite Wat Arun, is the historic center of the city, containing the Grand Palace and Wat Pho. This is the most attractive part of Bangkok, much visited, of course, by tourists, but an area of relative peace compared with the rest of the city.

The Administrative Area

Not far to the north stands the Democracy Monument, erected in memory of Thailand's first constitution, agreed to in 1932. This marks the southern end of the administrative area of the city where most of the government offices are situated. The Bangkok office of TAT, well-spring of almost all the informa-

tion you could possibly require for touring both the capital and the country, is close by. Close to the monument itself is Khaosarn Road, the Mecca of budget travelers seeking cheap accommodation in the city. And just to the north, adjacent to the Dusit Zoo, stands the National Assembly building. The wide street leading up to its façade is the venue for major national military parades on occasions such as the King's Birthday.

Some way to the east is **Sukhumvit Road**, the major up-market residential

area of the capital, and also a nightlife district. And away to the south, on the other side of Lumpini Park, is the **Silom and Surawong Road** district, the city's premier nightlife area.

MAJOR COMMUNICATIONS

Three major roads run east-west through the capital. From north to south, they are: (1) **Petchburi Road**, becoming **New Petchburi Road**, both of which can be numbered among the foulest urban highways on the planet; (2) **Rama I Road**, briefly becoming **Phloen Jhit Road**, then finally becoming **Sukhumvit Road**.

Rama I Road passes Siam Square on its south side, home to several major cinemas. Phloen Jhit Road is where several big department stores are located, while Sukhumvit Road houses, in its many long sois, almost all the luxury residences and exclusive restaurants in the capital. And (3), **Rama 4 Road**, passing the Snake Farm, the Dusit Thani Hotel (and statue of Rama the Fourth himself opposite), Lumpini Park and the Lumpini Boxing Stadium — all except the hotel on the north side —

Shrine on the corner on the right where it meets Rama I Road, with MacDonald's and the Sogo Department Store just round the same corner; and (4), **Wireless Road**, with its many embassies.

Bordered by Ratchadamri Road, Rama 4 Road and Wireless Road is **Lumpini Park**, the only large park in the center of the city.

South of Rama 4 Road, four important roads run southwest towards the river — **Surawong** and **Silom** roads, and **Sathorn**

before meeting Sukhumvit Road several kilometers further west.

Each of these three arterial roads runs underneath the **Express Way** which carries through traffic north to south across the city, and without which, ugly though it is, Bangkok would certainly have ceased operating altogether some years ago.

Four important roads run north to south and link Rama I and Rama 4 in the central area. From the west, they are : (1) **Phaya Thai Road**, a major bus route which has the Mah Boon Krong Department Store on the corner on the left where it meets Rama I Road; (2) **Henri Dunant Road**; (3) **Ratchadamri Road**, with the Erawan

Nua and **Sathorn Tai** roads. Between the first two lies the world-famous nightlife area of Patphong, centered on Patphong Road. In addition, there is a tourist-oriented informal night-market along the end of Silom nearest Rama 4 specializing in counterfeit-brand-name clothes, watches etc. The two Sathorn roads, each one-way, constitute an in-city throughway with few commercial premises.

Moving with confidence into a prosperous future? Holding the balance between army, king and people? Thai Government ministers in procession in Bangkok on the occasion of King Bhumipol's sixtieth birthday.

Surawong and Silom intersect with **New Road** — a street running parallel with and a few hundred meters from the river. Between the river and the road is an attractive area containing the Oriental, Shangri-la and Royal Orchid Sheraton hotels (plus the much cheaper Swan Hotel), and the old Portuguese Embassy.

WHERE TO STAY

Now you have got some idea of the basic lay-out of Bangkok's central area, and before setting out to take a look at it in more detail, you'll need to decide on somewhere to stay.

There are naturally a great many hotels and guest-houses in the Thai capital, and all it's feasible to do here is list a few in each price category. The main aim to is assist those arriving on their own without having accommodation booked in advance through travel or tour agents.

The **Oriental** (℃ 236 0400; fax: 236-1939; 394 rooms; rates: expensive) claims to be the best hotel in town, but the **Shangri-la** (℃ 236 7777; fax: 236 8579-80; 700 rooms; rates: expensive) is at least as good. These and the **Royal Orchid Sheraton** (℃ 234 5599; fax: 236 8320; 775 rooms; rates: expensive) are all on the river. Facing Lumpini Park stands the **Dusit Thani** (℃ 236 0450-9; fax: 236 6400; 525 roms; rates: expensive), while the **Regent** (℃ 251 6127; fax: 253 9195; 400 rooms; rates: expensive) is on Ratchadamri Road. The **Meridian President** (℃ 2530444; fax: 253 7565; 400 rooms; rates: expensive) and the **Landmark** (℃ 254 0404; fax: 253 4259; 415 rooms; rates: expensive) are on Phloen Jhit and Sukhumvit roads respectively.

Rather less expensive is the **Ambassador** (℃ 254 0444; fax: 253 4123; 935 rooms; rates: average and above) further down Sukhumvit in the middle of a restaurant and entertainment complex. On the other side of town, not far from the Grand Palace, is the old but atmospheric **Royal** (℃ 222 9111-26; fax: 224 2083; 297 rooms; rates: moderate).

There are a number of hotels at the river end of Suriwong and Silom roads, the **Narai** (℃ 237 0100-39; fax: 236 7161; 480 rooms; rates: average and above), the **New Peninsular** (℃ 234 53910-7; fax: 236-5526; 113 rooms; rates: average and above) and, nearer Patphong Road, the **Montien** (℃ 233 7060; fax: 236 55219; 500 rooms; rates: expensive).

The **Y.M.C.A.** (℃ 287 2727; fax: 287-1996; 147 rooms; rates: moderate) is very good value. Cheaper again are the **Reno Hotel** (℃ 215 0026-7) on Soi Kasemsan 1, off Rama 1, the **Sukhumvit Crown** (℃ 253 8401) on Sukhumvit Soi 8, and the **Swan** (℃ 2348594), close to the Oriental.

Close to the Swan is the **Executive Penthouse** (℃ 235 2642; rates: moderate; telex: 87476 TMENG TH) where rooms can be rented by the month or by the day.

As for the budget category, everything you could desire can be found in **Khaosarn Road**, close to the Democracy Monument on Rajdamnern Klang Road. This and neighboring streets contain a mass of family-run establishments, usually over a small restaurant. The clientele is almost exclusively non-Thai, and the restaurants specialize in all the things back-packers like to eat at home or away from home. Despite this foreign invasion, these are very Thai places — you leave your shoes at the foot of the stairs, and the family provides you with hot water in a vacuum flask. Rates are around two US dollars a night for a clean room, rarely with air-conditioning. The ambiance is congenial, with much exchanging of information and late-night chatting in cafes. There's a food market close by, and clothes stalls. It's reasonably quiet, too, at least after midnight — a rare quality in Bangkok.

The Parliament Building in Bangkok, covered in lights for King Bhumipol's sixtieth birthday. Prominent monuments all over the capital were decorated in this way. Scandals ensued over the misdirection of funds raised for the purpose, but for several weeks Bangkok shone like somewhere out of fairy-land.

It's also very easy to rent flats or rooms for extended periods. Establishments advertise every day in both the Bangkok Post and The Nation (the latter claiming to give up-to-the-minute occupancy levels). These places are rarely full, and it is possible to take accommodation for very short periods, so there's no difficulty in changing if you feel dissatisfied with where you've opted for. Some differ scarcely at all from hotel rooms with attached bathrooms; others, by contrast, have the aura of

endlessly re-used love-nests.

DINING IN STYLE

Bangkok, with its large foreign community and huge, year-round tourist influx, has a very wide range of restaurants, many of them superb. The serious gourmet should invest in a copy of the *Bangkok Restaurant Guide,* published in Thailand by Asia Books in an English/Thai parallel text edition. Their claim that it could pay for itself in one meal is probably justified, depending of course on the meal.

On the River
Some of the nicest places to eat are by the river. These must begin with the world-famous, and very expensive, **Normandie**, (236 0400, in the Oriental Hotel — French cuisine in a dining-room imitating the restaurant car of the old Orient Express. Also expensive, and huge, is the **Baan Khun Luang**, (241 0521, serving Thai food in several rooms. More reasonably priced is the **Banya**, (437 7329, opposite the Oriental — the restaurant will send a boat for you from the Oriental's or the Shangri-la's pier. Lastly, and nicest of all, is the **Maharaj**, (221 9073, situated at the stop of the same name on the regular Express Boat service. The food is Thai, not Indian, and there's traditional Thai music from 7 to 9 pm.

Rama I — Lumpini ParkLumpini Park
In the central area there are several good restaurants. Along Soi Langsuan (running from almost opposite the President Hotel to Lumpini Park) **Paesano 1**, (251 7104, serves good Italian food, while further down, on the other side of the road, **Whole Earth**, (252 5574, serves vegetarian and other Thai food. Just past the Whole Earth, on the corner opposite the park, is the **Ngwanlee Lungsuan**, (251 8366. Here cheap and excellent Chinese and Thai food is on offer in a dining room that is partly open-air (with a sliding roof for use during wet weather).

And for dining in high style, the Regent Hotel on Ratchadamri Road, parallel with Soi Langsuan, has its French cuisine **La Brasserie**, (2516127, and Thai **Spice Market**, (251 6603. At lunch time in the former you can enjoy a buffet of the highest order for a little over 200 baht.

Sukhumvit Road
The sois off Sukhumvit Road are thronged with classy restaurants, getting more lavish as the soi numbers rise. There's only room to mention three, one outstanding, and two less ambitious but deservedly popular. **Lemongrass**, (2588637, on Soi 24 is famous for serving sumptuous Thai food in authentic old-world surroundings. On Sukhumvit Road itself, on the corner of Soi 33, and very near Elite Books, **Pan Pan**, (258 9304, is a

Bangkok scenes – ABOVE: roofs of Wat Saket (The Golden Mount Temple). Constructed during the reign of Rama I (1782–1809), this temple affords fine views of the capital. Its golden *chedi* contains relics of the Lord Buddha. OPPOSITE: The waterfront on the Chao Phraya river with Wat Pho in the background.

very charming Italian cafe-restaurant. Finally, further back up the road towards the center of town, **By Otto**, (242 6836, serves traditional German food with great relish.

Also in this district, very close to Pan Pan, is the **Thai-French Co. Ltd.**, (258 5063, a combined butcher and cake-shop, and one of the most unexpected shops anywhere in Asia.

Just off Soi 3 here is a fine Egyptian restaurant, the **Nasir Al-Masri** ((253 5582) — it stays open till 3 am. (See also under **Vegetarian**, below)

Patphong
Good French food in intimate surroundings is at **La Paloma** ((233 3853) on Mahaesak Road, down towards New Road. The **Cafe India** ((234 1720), opposite the Trocadero Hotel on Surawong Road, is close by.

Show Restaurants
For a show of Thai classical dancing along with the meal, try the **Sala Rim Nam**, (437 6211, on the river (Thonburi bank) or the **Ruen Thep**, (235 8760, in the Silom Village Trade Center on Silom Road.

Vegetarian
Thai Buddhism is not the non-meat-eating variety, but vegetarians can find the food they require with a little trouble. Apart from the Whole Earth restaurant (see above), there is the **Mah Boon Krong** department store, near Silom Square. Here there is a wide selection of food stalls on the top floor, including one vegetarian one (but it does close in the early evening). There are others on the ground floor of the **Mall** department store, and in the **Ram Food Center**, both inexpensive but rather out on a limb from tourists' Bangkok on Ramkhamheng Road. The one place in Bangkok to go to find vegetarian food in abundance is in the vicinity of **Wat Santiasoke**.

There are also a number of Indian restaurants serving vegetarian meals — the superb **Moghul Room**, (253 6989, on Soi 11, off Sukhumvit Road (opposite the Ambassador Hotel), the rather less expensive **Akbar's**, (253 3479, on Sukhumvit Soi 3, and the **Shaharazade**, (251 3666, on the same soi.

Fast Food
There is an increasing number of outlets for American fast food, concentrated in the major shopping and commercial areas. There are several **MacDonald's** (expensively smart places to the average Thai), for example on Phloen Jhit and

Silom roads. There are **Dunkin' Donuts** and other scarcely distinguishable establishments on Rama 1 (between the cinemas fronting Siam Square) and at the top (Dusit Thani) end of Silom Road.

Doing it Yourself
The supermarket where the resident Westerners buy their delicacies is the **Villa Market**, close to Sio 33 on Sukhumvit Road.

GETTING TO KNOW THE CITY

Bangkok's attractions are best seen area by area. In this way, transport difficulties can be kept to a minimum. You can walk between sites, or, in the case of those accessible by water, take a delightful trip on one of the river boats.

THE GRAND PALACE AND WAT PHO

Bangkok's **Grand Palace,** and **Wat Phra Kheo,** within its grounds, were established in 1782 with the foundation of the Chakri dynasty, and the promulgation of Bangkok as the Thai capital in succession to Thonburi on the other side of the river.

But it isn't all show. Splendor is combined with serenity, and worldly display blended with spiritual confidence in an impregnable unity.

The sumptuousness and extravagance, which seems so unrestrained to Western taste, is actually blended with an elegance that is quite as sophisticated as anything in Europe's bastions of culture, in Vienna, Paris or Venice. And in fact much of it is European — the classical courtyards and administrative buildings that flank the temple

Anything more like a fairy palace, a magic castle of dreams, it's difficult to imagine. It's too gorgeous, too colorful to be true — it must be a dream, a vision of true ecstasy and happiness.

And it really does have the power to cause you to exult in its presence. Maybe that was what it was designed to do in the first place.

From time to time *son et lumiere* shows are staged here, but they tend to be rather disappointing because what this kind of architecture needs above all is the glory and power of the sun. In the brilliant Thai sunlight, the multicolored mosaics and soaring gold stupas intoxicate with their sheer, unambiguous splendor.

Bangkok and Ayutthaya

are imported nineteenth century state architecture in style. The Grand Palace has, combined with its magnificence, something of the quiet elegance of the colonnades of Aix en Provence or Verona.

The Emerald Buddha

Wat Phra Kheo is better known as the Temple of the Emerald Buddha and con-

A general view of the Thai capital. Note ABOVE the combination of high-rises and the more traditional, and older, two-story buildings. (The really traditional, wooden houses are largely confined these days to the river- and canal-side areas). OPPOSITE: A Garland-seller; fragrant chains of jasmine hang in most taxis and some tuk-tuks.

tains a green image that it's forbidden to photograph and that is held to be linked to the very continuance of the Chakri dynasty itself. This is typical of the magical power attributed to sacred objects world-wide, and in this case the Buddha's supreme potency long predates the supremacy of the current Thai royal family. Its recorded history alone goes back to the fifteenth century, since when it has been fought over by contenders for power in many parts of South-East Asia. To this day the Thai monarch in person ritually changes the little early Chakri period cloaks the image wears, a different one for each of the three Thai seasons.

Admission to the complex is 100 baht during the week, free on Saturdays and Sundays (but on these two days the temple containing the Emerald Buddha is closed). Hours are from 8:30 to 11:30 am and 1 to 3:30 pm. Formal dress is essential — no shorts.

Wat Pho

Wat Pho is Bangkok's oldest and grandest temple, and contains Thailand's largest Reclining Buddha (46m (150 ft) long and 15m (49 ft) high). It's also one of those monuments scattered round the world which the continual presence of masses of tourists effectively deprives of much of the atmosphere the visitors came to sample in the first place. You are yourself that which you most resent. From this paradox there is, unfortunately, no known escape.

One solution is to go early in the morning, soon after sunrise. Then, with luck, you will see this large temple more or less as it was intended to be experienced.

The temple is divided into two halves by Jetuphon Road; one half is taken up with the monks' quarters. The features you might choose to photograph in the other, public, section are the large chedis in the courtyard (either containing the ashes of or commemorating the country's first four kings of the modern dynasty), the inlaid mother-of-pearl soles of the Reclining Buddha's feet, the beautiful reliefs from Ayutthaya round the base of the main

bot (often seen as rubbings on sale all over the city), the painted teak shutters in the hall containing the giant Buddha, and the traditional medical practitioners who still dispense treatment daily in the main compound. Many features of the temple were extensively restored to mark the King's 60th birthday in 1988.

The Reclining Buddha itself is made of brick, covered in cement and then finally covered with gold leaf. It was constructed during the reign of Rama III in about 1824. Like all reclining Buddhas, it depicts the great teacher's last position before death. You won't be admitted to the great hall containing the statue after 5 pm.

THE RIVER

The Chao Phraya River represents Bangkok's only major contact with nature, and consequently is far and away the most congenial feature of the city.

But it's also an important highway, both nationally and within the capital. The Chao Phraya Express Boat Service is the most efficient means of traveling between two points on the river's course, and it's also easily the pleasantest way to get about anywhere in the city.

Oriental Hotel

Begin at the **Oriental Hotel Pier**. Before embarking on a river boat, you could take a walk round the nearby area, one of the least changed in Bangkok, and perhaps take a snack on the hotel's **riverside terrace**, not cheap, but one of the most congenial places in the city. The hotel itself is worth a look, too. It's one of Bangkok's oldest, and though the newer section now dominates the scene, the old part — closest to the pier — is still in use. The hotel has many literary associations,

The famous Reclining Buddha in Bangkok's Wat Pho. Recently re-decorated, the gigantic figure now glitters in great splendor. You can walk round it and examine the revered presence from every angle. The soles of its feet are particularly noteworthy.

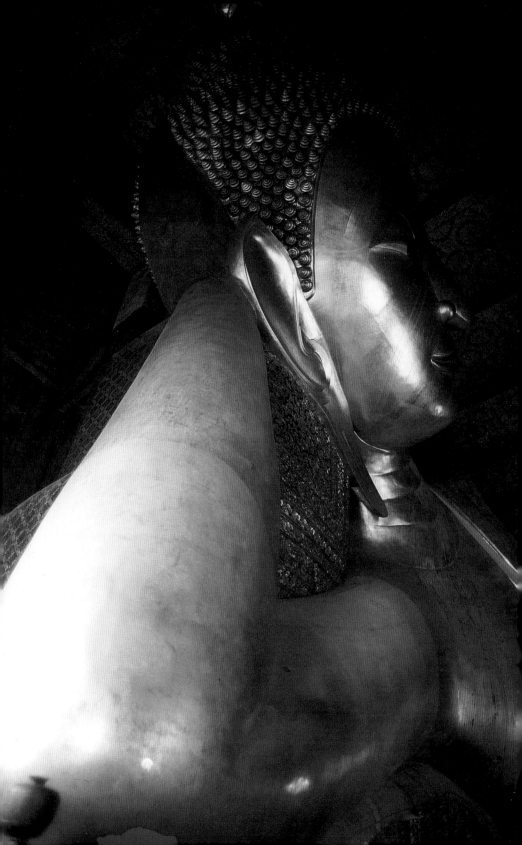

something the management makes perhaps rather too much of, but at least you'll have information to hand when you're there about who stayed there when, and so on.

The Express Boat

Back at the Pier, just say "Express Boat" and you'll be shown where to wait. You want one going to the right, i.e. up-river. Once on-board, take a seat and someone will come round and collect your

in return expected not to occupy seats. At some Express Boat landing stages you are required to hand back your ticket, with a 50 stang fine if you can't find it. As the monks never have tickets, a special gate exists to let them out without their having to pass through the turnstile. This gate is operated at the push of a button by the attendant and is a comically elaborate mechanism to enable the continued operation of the principle of monastic poverty in modern conditions. Its essential purpose, of course, is

fare. Charges vary according to where you're going, so you should read on and decide in advance where it is you want to get off.

For Wat Pho or Wat Arun, ask for a ticket to Tha Tien.

A Monks' Gate

You will notice that almost all the Express Boats have monks standing at the back in a group. If you ask them, they will say the reason for this is that they are not permitted by their monastic rules to sit next to or near women, but the real reason is probably that monks travel free of charge on all Bangkok transport, and are

to avoid a situation where the attendant can let people through the turnstile without paying the 50 stang fine at her own discretion, and hence open the way for corruption.

Tha Tien

To begin with the Express Boat keeps to the right hand bank, and continues to do so for some way after passing under the first bridge (the Memorial Bridge). Note the plants floating down the river — they're water hyacinths and exist naturally in this state. After the bridge, look out for the Tha Tien stop, and get off there. Tha Tien is the stop for **Wat Pho**,

— see under GRAND PALACE and WAT PHO above (p. 59) for details of this famous temple.

Before leaving the waterside, take a glance at the small **Market** immediately behind the landing-stage. It seems to specialize in dried fish, and can hardly have changed since Conrad's day.

Wat Arun

Wat Arun is most conveniently reached from the Tha Tien landing-stage. There's

city, with the river in the foreground, from the highest accessible point.

Wat Arun is a quiet place, much photographed from the river and seen as a symbol of Bangkok, but little visited. It's a good place to relax.

Maharaj Restaurant

By now you'll no doubt be feeling hungry, so it's a quick trip back to Tha Tien, and then two more stops up-river on the Express Boat before getting off at the stop

little to see (in contrast to Wat Pho), but the trip involves fresh air and gardens, and a superb lunch can be conveniently enjoyed immediately afterwards.

A ferry will take you over to the temple — enquire at Tha Tien. There is no Express Boat stop.

Named after Aruna, Indian god of the dawn, this Temple of the Dawn essentially consists of a simple *prang*, or gracefully tapering tower, in this case embedded with pieces of broken porcelain. It stands in rather attractively neglected gardens, and you can climb to half way up via some extremely steep steps (easier to go up than down). You get an excellent view over the

named **Maharaj**.

Here lunch awaits you at the very fine restaurant of the same name as the landing-stage. As described in the DINING IN STYLE (p.56) section, the **Maharaj Restaurant** is one of the nicest places to eat in the city. Situated right on the river, it's beautiful, charming and not particularly expensive. It is not haute cuisine, but with its flowering plants and rose table-

Two faces of Bangkok — LEFT: the lobby of the Oriental Hotel, one of the world's most celebrated hostelries; ABOVE: barges on the Chao Phraya River. The Oriental has a famous terrace restaurant where the comfortably-off can observe the busy life of the river.

en Buddhas line the cloisters, with memorial plaques to the recently dead, plus their photographs, at their feet. Cats and dogs pace about with a slowness that is both deliberate and casual. Small groups of Thais chat softly round a venerated tree, the pink and yellow ribbons round its trunk fluttering in the light breeze. Some lie in the shade asleep, stirring slightly as a bell rings high up under the eaves.

cloths, (and Thai classical music in the evenings), it constitutes an essential ingredient of any Bangkok river-trip.

Wat Mahatar

After lunch, you'll probably feel like nothing more arduous than one last temple, and then a leisurely look at the **Royal Barges**.

Wat Mahatar stands across the street that runs past the Maharaj Restaurant. This street, incidentally, is famous for its lines of stalls selling ancient amulets and other pendants. The monastery is far less touristed than Wa Po, and is actually the premises of the Mahachulalongkorn Buddhist University so casual visitors are not encouraged. Nevertheless, you can slip in if you're discreet.

Immediately the atmosphere of quiet greets you. Pigeons flutter in the forecourt, and palm trees cast insufficient shade on orange tiles. Rows upon rows of dusty gold-

Inside in a lecture hall, the silence is absolute and only one fan in a dozen turns, like a prayer-wheel. Boy monks are watching English football on TV in the vestry.

You can walk through the temple compound and exit onto Phra Chan Road. At the gate you can buy a religious picture, a *memento mori* Thai-style, almost Surrealist in its iconography, depicting a pair of lovers aging, dying, and finally becoming skeletons, locked in a harsh parody of their youthful embraces.

The Royal Barges

From Wat Mahatar you can get to the **Royal Barges**, situated up a creek on the Thonburi side of the river, either by going back to the Maharaj landing-stage and

---

Golden Bangkok — ABOVE: the Standing Buddha of Wat Indrawihan (on Thanon Wisut Kasat in Bangkhunphrom), often called "Laung Pho To" after its builder; ABOVE RIGHT and OPPOSITE LEFT: in the Temple of the Emerald Buddha; OPPOSITE RIGHT: roofs at Wat Pho, each with its horn-shaped *chofa*.

arranging water-transport, or by taking a tuk-tuk across Phrapinklao Bridge, getting off as soon as the bridge road descends to ordinary ground level.

If you do the latter, you should double back towards the river left of the bridge. The way is then well signposted in English, and leads you through a mass of wooden Thai houses, thereby giving you an insight into the lifestyle and living conditions of many Bangkok citizens it might be difficult to find otherwise.

The barges, ceremonial vessels for carrying the monarch along the river on state occasions, are housed in a large modern boathouse, looking like an aircraft hangar. There are eight of them, the longest 49 m (160 ft) long, all gorgeously decorated in

red, black and gold, with rigid flags and fantastically carved prows. One old one is cut up into sections to reveal its structure. The boathouse closes at 4:30 pm. (See MORE RIVER TRIPS (p. 70).

OTHER TEMPLES

Wat Benchamabophit

Situated on Sri Ayuthaya Road, near

Dusit Zoo, this is a very beautiful place. With its white Italian Carrara marble, orange Chinese tiles, very un-Thai stained glass (made in Florence), carved doors, embossed and gorgeously painted ceilings, this small temple encapsulates late nineteenth century Thai royal eclecticism. King Chulalongkorn embraced the West, and in this ornate yet oddly straightforward place, he brought all the glory of Italy to join hands with Thai piety and Thai splendor.

It was completed in 1899, and a portion of King Chulangkorn's ashes were laid to rest under the revered central Buddha image.

Wat Traimit

This temple, situated near Hualamphong Station, at the intersection of Yaowarat and Charoen Krung roads, is without architectural or atmospheric interest but contains something difficult to believe in, a statue of the Buddha made out of *five and a half tonnes* of solid gold.

The gold is claimed to be 18 carat, or 80 percent pure. It's assumed, on account of its style, to date from the Sukhothai

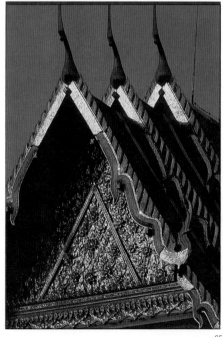

period. The image was for a long time covered by plaster, and its true nature was only discovered when it was dropped by a crane while being moved in 1953. It can only have been plastered over to disguise it from enemies in time of invasion, possibly during one of the attacks on Ayutthaya by the Burmese. Why the plaster was not removed when the danger receded — unless all the defenders in on the secret were killed — remains a mystery.

The image is about 3 m (10 ft) high, and the buildings that house them. The Vejayany-Raja-Roth, a royal funeral chariot standing in a room crowded with many others, is itself worth the entrance fee. Reconstructions of scenes from Thai history (in the first pavilion you come to) are, on the other hand, less impressive.

As is often the case in Thailand, taking photos of venerable objects is not allowed for fear the resulting pictures might be used in unbecoming contexts (or take away some of the sanctity of the thing photographed).

and stands incongruously against a pink, gloss-painted wall.

CULTURAL ATTRACTIONS

The National Museum
To get to the **National Museum**, leave the Grand Palace by the main gate, cross the road and walk down Naphrathat Road, with the open grassy space known as Senam Luang on your right. You reach the museum entrance after passing along the front of Thammasat University.

The museum is vast, and very varied, not only in the items it contains, but also in the standard of their presentation, Guided tours to the museum in English are held on Tuesday, Wednesday and Thursday mornings, a different aspect of Thai culture being covered each day. Check with TAT for the up-to-date details.

The National Museum is open from 9 am to 4 pm daily, except Mondays and Fridays when it is closed. Admission is 20 baht.

The National Theater
Right next door to the museum is the **National Theater**.

This institution is not one dedicated to the best that is produced in the dramatic arts (as in some countries) so much as to regular displays of traditional dramatic forms. It's a big, Western style building of a kind now rather out-dated in the West, with a classical front and a vast, proscenium-arch auditorium. Should you wander in through a wrong door you are likely to stumble on dusty rooms, empty except for tribes of semi-domesticated cats.

Long historico-mythical court dramas (known as *khon*), based on stories from the Ramayana Indian epics and with instrumental and sung accompaniment, are staged in the main auditorium as follows — on the second weekend of the month: Friday at 5:30 pm, Saturday at 9:30 am, 2 and 6 pm, and Sunday at 9:30 am, 1 pm and 6 pm; on the fourth weekend of the month: Friday at 5:30 pm and Saturday at 1 pm only. Phone (224 1342 to confirm these details. Entrance is 100 and 200 baht.

More to the popular taste are outdoor performances given every Saturday and Sunday at 4:30 pm. The style presented varies each week. They're very much social events, with people spreading out mats and newspapers for picnics.

Senam Luang

This open space in front of the National Theater and National Museum is the venue for interesting events at the weekends — free concerts, rallies and even demonstrations. This is where the king performs the annual Ploughing Ceremony. Kites are also flown here, and are on sale on the pavement where Phrachan Road meets the open area. In the summer months, large kites are flown, sometimes sponsored by one of the beer or soft drinks companies. Nothing could be more restful than to watch these beautiful kites while you sit down and rest your feet.

The Siam Society

This society, under royal patronage, maintains premises on the main road known as Sukhumvit Soi 21 (Soi Asoke). There are exhibitions of folk art and a reference library. Open daily (except Sundays and Mondays) from 9 am to noon, then 1 to 5 pm.

Erawan Shrine

At the intersection of Rama I with Ratchadamri Road, you will see on one corner, diagonally opposite the site for the new World Trade Center, the Erawan Shrine, named after the sacred three-headed elephant of Buddhist iconography. This is a very important site for Thais — here requests are made, and devotional offerings promised should the request be granted. A troupe of somewhat tired-looking classical Thai dancers perform dances for a fee as part of the said offerings. The shrine stands in the grounds of the former Erawan Hotel; the old colonial hotel's modern successor, the Grand Hyatt Erawan, is now being constructed on the same site.

Jim Thompson's House

Open every day except Sundays, from 9 am to 5 pm, this was the home of a rich American who decided to settle in Thailand after the war and put his mind and resources to reinvigorating the Thai silk industry. His disappearance in the Cameron Highlands of Malaysia in 1967 has never been explained.

The attraction of the house — actually six fine old wooden buildings put together to make one — is that, in a country awash with Coca Cola and the Snoopy culture, it is a real oasis of traditional Thai art. It's even worth the 100 baht entrance fee, and the often protracted wait for a guide. Most of all, it is an example of tropical luxury as it was in the old, pre-air-conditioned days. It's infinitely more beautiful than anything modern day 5-star Thailand can offer.

The house is full of the most wonderful objects from Burma, Cambodia, China

OPPOSITE: The giant *chedi* on Wat Saket (the Golden Mount Temple). This glittering structure dominates the skyline of the west-central area of the Thai capital.

and Thailand — the hard-working guides will tell you all you want to know about them, plus a great deal more. Thompson's silk factories were situated on the opposite bank of the klong, and you can still see newly-dyed silk from the few workshops that remain there being dried in the sun.

The house stands in an idyllic setting on Soi Kasem San 2, off Rama I Road, a world away from modern Bangkok's traffic nightmare. The quiet little garden by the klong, empty of art objects, is almost more beautiful than the house; nature, as usual, has the last word. Entrance to this garden is free of charge.

A Bangkok Klong

Before you brace yourself to face the main road, turn left as you leave the garden and go down towards the klong. To inspect the silk factories, and see at first hand the living conditions of many of Bangkok's ordinary residents, cross the klong by a small punt that will come over to fetch you (fare: 5 baht). To summon this boat, just stand on the bank and wave.

SUKHUMVIT ROAD

Ploen Jhit continues under the Express Way, and over a railway track. It then becomes Sukhumvit Road. The **Regal Landmark Hotel** is on the right, and opposite are many small shops and kerbside stalls dealing in craft wares, traveling bags and clothing for the tourist trade. This is also one of Bangkok's main nightlife areas — the **Grace Hotel** off to the left down Soi 3 (Soi Nana) and the **Nana Hotel** on the same soi to the right of the road, are central to the pleasure scene.

Next on the left is the **Ambassador Hotel**, with its attendant restaurants in the extensive forecourt between the hotel and the road. And finally, when you've passed the wide road leading off to the left — Soi 21 (Soi Asoke) — you quickly reach the attractive sois in the thirties, and the particularly charming huddle, near Soi 33,

of the **Pan Pan** cafe/restaurant, the **Thai-French Co. Ltd.** (see SUKHUMVIT ROAD under DINING IN STYLE p.56) and Bangkok's best second-hand bookstore for non-Thai volumes, **Elite Books**.

IN THE SNAKE PIT

The premises of the Thai Red Cross are in two parts, one on either side of Henri Dunant Road where it joins Rama 4 Road. The part that houses the Snake Farm is on

your right coming out of Henri Dunant. Alternatively, it's a short walk from Robinson's department store at the top of Silom Road, or the nearby Dusit Thani Hotel.

The public display of snake-handling and sample extraction of venom takes place every morning, except public holidays, at 11 am. Entry is 40 baht for foreigners, 20 baht for Thais.

OPPOSITE: Offerings at Bangkok's Erawan shrine. Situated at a busy traffic intersection, it is not the most charming venue for the curious visitor, but it is very important to all Thais. ABOVE: Jim Thompson's House, Bangkok — a far more restful place for the foreigner, though a lot less significant to the locals than the shrine.

The farm was established in 1923 and its purpose is to produce anti-snake-bite serum, for use at home and overseas.

The display takes place on two sides of an area of grass and water where the snakes are kept. The audience is divided into two, and two virtually identical displays take place simultaneously — presumably an arrangement to create space for the large proportion of tourists wanting to take photographs.

To begin with the snakes are just held up and goaded lightly to encourage them to behave in ways that the keepers know the visitors will think photogenic. It's all very amiable, and almost unrehearsed, like so many things in Asia.

Then the small amount of venom — maybe two thirds of a gram — is extracted from a couple of cobras, through their very large fangs into a small circular glass dish. But it's powerful stuff — enough to kill a thousand rabbits, or a significant number of human beings.

The snakes themselves are, of course, the real objects of wonder, rather than their keepers. They're immensely beautiful in their lithe, sinuous movement, as they elegantly coil themselves into spirals and then raise their proud heads to hiss.

Afterwards, a twelve foot python is draped round the neck of anyone interested in the experience. Friends' cameras click — and for some reason it always seems to be the women who are especially anxious to volunteer.

THAI BOXING

There are two main places to see Thai boxing in central Bangkok.

Next to the TAT office on Ratchadamnoen Avenue is the **Ratchadamnoen Stadium**, the most important venue for the

activity. Boxing here takes place on Mondays, Wednesdays, Thursdays and Sundays, beginning at 6 pm (5 pm on Sundays).

On the other days of the week, Tuesdays, Fridays and Saturdays, the bouts are at **Lumpini Stadium**, on Rama 4 Road, a few hundred meters west of the corner of the park at the junction of Rama 4 and Wireless roads. Lumpini Stadium is described, along with the whole business of Thai boxing, in A NIGHT AT THE RINGSIDE section on P.37. It is the more atmospheric of the two venues and the one to attend to get the flavor of this quintessentially Thai activity.

There are three price categories — ringside at 500 baht, second class at 240 baht, and third class at 120 baht.

MORE RIVER TRIPS

In addition to the tour along the river described above, there are other trips you can take.

(1) To **Klong Mon**. Boats start from Tha Tien Pier, near Wat Pho.

(2) To **Klong Bang Waek**. Boats leave from the Memorial Bridge Pier.

(3) To **Klong Bang Khoo Wiang** and **Klong Bang Yai**. Boats leave from Tha Chang Pier, near the Grand Palace.

These trips cost only a few baht and take you to untouristed parts of the city. They're recommended.

FLOATING MARKETS

The problem with these early morning markets where vegetables and fruit are sold off boats is that the easily accessible one is nowadays extremely full of tourists, and the other one is 80 km (50 miles) out of town.

To get to the more accessible **Wat Sai** market, either join one of the very numerous coach parties heading there (any travel agent will book you onto one), or catch one of the boats going there that leave the Oriental Hotel Pier at 7 am every morning.

The Amarin Center, Bangkok. American-style department stores are increasingly common in the Thai capital, and the introduction of non-Asian architectural styles has attracted some criticism. But "exotic" means "foreign" in Thailand, as elsewhere.

To get to the slightly more authentic version at **Damnoen Saduak** in Ratchaburi Province, again either join a tour, or catch a public bus there from the Southern Bus Terminal on Charansanitwong Road any time between 5 and 8:30 am.

WEEKEND MARKET

This is a very extensive market held every Saturday and Sunday from 7 am to 6 pm. There are sections specializing in everything from house plants to caged birds, shirts to dinner plates. It's situated up the Phahonyothin Road, on a corner of Chatuchak Park opposite the Northern Bus terminal.

LUMPINI PARK

This is the only open space in the city other than the river. It's not at all a bad place, reasonably extensive and with a large lake where you can hire boats. At the end of the afternoon hundreds of joggers arrive — it's the only place in the city where they can exercise in peace.

At 6 pm the Thai national anthem strikes up from loudspeakers and everyone stands at attention. You should do the same, or at least stand still and stop talking. Thais on the lake even try to bring their boats to a standstill. The park closes at 7 pm.

CHINATOWN

Near the intersection of Ratchawong Road and Yaowaraj Road to the west of Hualumphong Railway Station lies Bangkok's Chinatown. In the narrow side-streets everything from antiques to joss-sticks is for sale. The so-called Thieves' Market — ask for Woeng Nakhon Kasem — is also nearby. It specializes in antiques and objets d'art.

And out in the northern suburbs, on Soi Sukson 7, near Lard Phrao Road, is an attractive temple well-known to Chinese both in Thailand and elsewhere, the **Kuan-Im Palace.**

NIGHT LIFE

Bangkok is so much a center of nightlife, and, quite simply, sex, the subject deserves a book all on its own. It so happens a compact little guide has been published by the present publisher — *Bangkok by Night* by Lee Daniel covers all most men, at least, will want to know about the very extensive action after dark.

While you're looking around for a copy, a trip out to the **Nasa Spacedrome** on Suapa Road, (221 1685, offers you the experience of what the owners claim is the biggest and most lavish disco in the world.

The three main Bangkok nightlife "strips" are: (1) **Patphong Road**, between Silom and Suriwong roads; (2) **Soi Cowboy**, between Sukhumvit sois 21 and 23; and (3) **Nana Plaza and adjacent area** on Sukhumvit Soi 4 (Soi Nana). Between them they will provide you with enough live-shows and sex by the hour to last you what's left of a lifetime.

As for **Massage Parlors**, they're all over the city. They're usually called "Turkish Bath and Massage" in English and offer, of course, massage and more. Some are vast, multi-storeyed establishments staffed by hundreds of girls. To find one, simply consult the Yellow Pages classified phone book (there's an English version) under Massage. The biggest parlors in town are probably the **Atami** and the **Mona Lisa** on New Petchburi Road.

section, you will see, on the corner on your right, the **Mah Boon Krong** department store.

Go inside and marvel at the anomalies revealed in Thailand's headlong rush towards modernization. The building is half department store, half frenetic market, with everything from numerous stalls competing to sell cheap cassettes to one offering very expensive cups of real coffee.

A little way further down Rama I is the

For simple massage, by the way, look for the sign "Ancient Massage". This means traditional, therapeutic massage, which is not to imply the other sort isn't therapeutic too. It doesn't, or at least not necessarily, mean "massage by ancient ladies" as one Thai friend assured me that it did.

SHOPPING

Many of the big department stores are situated on Rama I Road. If, beginning at Jim Thompson's House, you walk back onto Rama I, then turn left and proceed until you arrive at the first inter-

Siam Center, on your left. It's a collection of up-market boutiques, a large number of coffee-shops, some with live music and mostly on the top floor, and the American Express Clients' Mail office (in the Sea Tours agency).

On the opposite side of the road is **Siam Square**, a popular shopping and restaurant complex occupying a small

OPPOSITE and ABOVE: the Floating Market at Damnoen Suduak. This provincial early morning market is very picturesque, and somewhat less of a tourist magnet than the one in Bangkok (which is nowadays largely kept going by TAT specifically for the tourists' benefit).

grid of streets, not expensive but nevertheless with an international, non-Thai feel about it.

Not far past the Erawan Shrine, and next to MacDonald's, is the **Amarin Center**, containing **Sogo** department store. On the opposite side of the road stands the **President Hotel**, facing sideways into a square containing many restaurants serving Western food. A little way past the President and on the same side is a large branch of the **Central** department store. Another big store is **Robinson's**, at the junction of Silom and Rama IV roads. All stores stay open till around 8 pm.

For an array of items thought to be especially attractive to tourists — leatherware and traveling bags especially — the top end of Sukhumvit Road, on the opposite side to the Regal Landmark Hotel, is a good bet. (From the President Hotel, continue down Ploen Jhit Road until you pass under the Expressway — and over a railway line — and you're there).

Thai silk can be purchased in many places in the capital, either in lengths or made up into garments. Sukhimvit Road, again, has many small retailers, and **Jim Thompson's Shop,** 9 Surawong Road, is the place to go for the internationally renowned Jim Thompson Silk.

Western-style **shopping arcades** can be found attached to the Oriental, President and the Ambassador hotels.

You can find **roadside vendors** just about anywhere in the city. Of particular interest to tourists are those along one side of Silom Road, close to Patpong. They operate from late afternoon until after midnight and specialize in cotton clothes, counterfeit watches, cassette tapes and various handicrafts.

In the so-called **Thieves' Market** (Nakhon Kasem) in Chinatown look for antiques and other traditional items. Chinatown is also the place to go if you're interested in buying gold.

TRANSPORT

Bangkok's morning rush-hour now lasts from shortly after dawn to just before lunch time. It resumes in mid-afternoon and doesn't really ease up till nine at night. At its twin heights, the times when most cities experience some problems, it's sometimes quickest simply to walk. Taxis can do little to by-pass the metal log-jam, and even the opportunistic tuk-tuks cannot always escape getting bogged down in the morass.

With only the briefest of pauses in the small hours of the night, a tide of trucks, vans, motorbikes, evil-smelling tuk-tuks, and hideously polluting buses snarl and shudder along the broad arterial highways. There is little lane discipline. Tuk-tuks weave in and out among the larger vehicles, taxis without a fare slow down or stop on catching sight of a foreigner, government vehicles bearing a single passenger pull out from side-roads and hold up thousands of others in the dark river of traffic. A blue-black haze rises to meet the merciless sun. The noise is appalling, and the air pollution leaves a foul taste in the mouth.

Bangkok is considering an aerial railway — the ground is too wet for a subway to be a viable option. Until its arrival, you must be content to negotiate the roads.

Your choice is simple — taxis, tuk-tuks or buses.

Taxis and Tuk-tuks

Taxis and tuk-tuks are rarely hard to come by — you're more likely to be pestered to take one when all you want to do is walk round the corner. No-one walks in Asia except the very poor, and a *farang* walking can only mean he can't find a taxi.

You must fix the fare before you move off. Bargain hard, but not unrealistically, with the drivers. Thais get everything cheaper, but if you want to get down to their price level you'll either have to learn some Thai or be extremely patient. And traffic conditions do count — to the driver, time is money, and it's how long it's going to take him to get you to where you want to go, rather than the simple distance, that is the relevant consideration.

Some average fares, in average traffic conditions, are as follows:

Oriental Hotel to Sukhumvit Road — 70 baht; Sukhumvit Road to Grand Palace

Buses

There are three kinds of bus running the Bangkok streets, the long blue and cream ones without curtains and with open doors, similar vehicles with curtains and doors that are shut except at stops, and the smaller, more modern micro-buses.

The curtained and closed-in buses are the air-conditioned ones. They can be recognized in advance by the Thai lettering before the route number on the front of

— 50 baht; President Hotel to Patphong — 30 baht; Silom Road to Democracy Monument — 55 baht.

A tuk-tuk is, as a rule, quicker than a taxi, if hair-raising. It also exposes you to the full force of exhaust-pollution, its own and everyone else's. A tuk-tuk costs in general around 25 percent less than a taxi.

It's worth knowing that no Thai tuk tuk or taxi-driver owns his vehicle. They hire them for 24-hour stints, two drivers each working 12 hours, and first have to work off the rental before they can make anything to feed themselves and their families.

the bus. Fares here depend on where you're going (though it's always possible to offer 5 baht if you're not sure) and you stand a reasonable chance of getting a seat.

The other two operate different versions of the same thing. The flat fare is two baht, rising to three baht after around 10 pm. All types of bus only stop if someone indicates they want to get on — otherwise free-flow situations in Bangkok's traffic

---

Charm mixes with nightmare on the streets of Bangkok. ABOVE: Bangkok's horendous traffic — note the tuk-tuk in the center desperately trying to change lanes.

are too good to miss. To stop a bus, just wave.

The micro-buses are much nicer inside, though they are a bit cramping if you're tall and have to stand. And they have music. So you can sit in the inevitable Bangkok traffic jam, watching fumes pour from the vehicles pulled up beside you, and listen to pop songs.

You will notice some of the big buses display their numbers on red or orange backgrounds in their front windows. Red

means "limited stop", and orange that they take a short-cut to their ultimate destination by using the Express Way. This latter can be most alarming if you encounter it unawares. Just when you're getting near your stop, the doors are fastened shut (where they're not rusted fast in the open position) and the vehicle hurtles for five or six miles at top speed along the elevated highway to an outer suburb. If you're caught in this way, the only thing is to get off at the first stop and take the next bus with the same number back in the direction from which you came.

Buses run all night on several routes. Your hotel should be able to provide you

Thai transport — ABOVE: longtail boat on the Chao Phraya River; OPPOSITE: a moderately full country taxi somewhere north of Chiang Rai. Additional examples might include the tuk-tuks (also known as *samlors*), the horse-drawn cabs of Lampang, and the pedicabs of the provincial towns.

with information on how to get back late from areas where you're likely to be enjoying yourself in the small hours.

GETTING OUT OF TOWN

There are two main railway stations in Bangkok. The biggest is **Hualamphong Station** on Rama 4, (223 0341-8. The other is over the river in Thonburi, **Bangkok Noi**, (223 0341 Ext. 713. Trains for Kanchanaburi and a few for the south leave from Thonburi. All others leave from Hualamphong. You must have reserved seats before you can travel, so make sure you book your tickets in advance, or get an agent or your hotel to do it for you.

For buses, there are three terminals. For Pattaya and the east coast it's **Ekamai** at Sukhumvit Soi 40, (391 2504, for the south it's **Charansanitwong** on the road of the same name, (411 4978-9, and for the north and northeast the **Northern Bus Terminal** on Phahonyothin Road, (2794484-7.

For transport between Bangkok and the airport, see the TRAVELERS' TIPS section.

TOURIST INFORMATION

The Tourism Authority of Thailand's national headquarters is on Ratchadamnoen Nok Avenue, (282 1143-7. They have an immense amount of information covering both Bangkok and the rest of the country. They're extremely efficient.

AROUND BANGKOK

CROCODILES AND ROSES

Samphran Elephant Ground and Zoo
Thirty kilometers (19 miles) west of Bangkok on the road to Nakhorn Phathom, this is best known for its crocodiles, and is often referred to simply as the Crocodile Farm.

Richard Clayderman and "A Stranger in Paradise" blare inescapably from the tannoy while elephants "dance" and play football

before raked stadium-style seating holding up to 500. This is followed by a "Crocodile Wrestling Show" which ends with the keeper putting his head in the crocodile's mouth — it stays open after he's walked away and has to be forcibly shut by assistants.

The elephant shows are at 1:30 pm (additional shows at 11:30 am and 3:30 pm on holidays), the crocodile shows at 12:30, 2:30 and 4:50 pm (with extra shows on holidays at 9:45 and 11:00 am).

Though the place is clearly popular with some, it's generally worth giving a miss unless you're with very young children.

The Rose Garden

A short way up the road from the Crocodile Farm is the large complex known as the **Rose Garden**. It's a good deal less dreadful, and a lot more peaceful.

The main feature is the "Thai Village" where, for an entrance fee of 140 baht, you can see various traditional crafts such as umbrella-making and pottery and then, at 2:15 and 3:15 pm daily, a Cultural Show featuring finger-nail dancing, hill-tribe dancing, Thai boxing, sword-fighting, a wedding, and elephants in procession. Short rides on the elephants are 20 baht extra. It's all packaged, of course, and consequently rather twee and unreal. But it's not bad as these things go.

A mere 10 baht will let you into the gardens themselves, laid out on the banks of the river and featuring some rose beds. The climate of the Bangkok region is not suited to rose-growing and such roses as there are here will not hold the attention of enthusiasts for long. Nevertheless, the attempt has been made, and the gardens

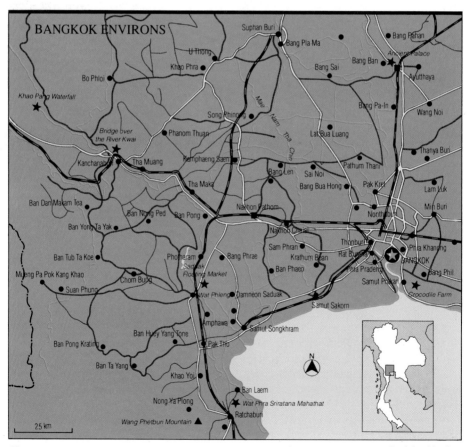

themselves are pleasant. There's also a lake with peddalos, pony-and-trap rides are available, and you can hire bicycles (10 baht for half an hour).

Much of this area is owned by the Roman Catholic Church and referred to by some as "Thailand's Vatican City". There are several seminaries nearby.

AYUTTHAYA AND BANG PA-IN

Ayutthaya (named after the city of Ayodhya in the ancient Indian romance, the *Ramayana*) is Thailand's main historical site, but it may, nevertheless, prove a disappointment to some visitors.

The ancient city, 72 km (45 miles) north of Bangkok, was the Thai capital from AD 1350 for over four hundred years. When the Burmese sacked it in 1767, the Thais established a new capital at Thonburi.

Ayutthaya was undoubtedly one of the greatest and most magnificent cities of the entire region. Today, however, it resembles a hive from which all the bees have departed. Brick ruins lean and gently crumble among carefully tended lawns, carved torsos in blackened stone lie in piles, and in the great heat gardeners hack out weeds from the tottering walls. Tourists ritually photograph the remains, locals on motorbikes putter about their business along the nearby by-pass, and a low breeze wafts across the vast, muddy plain.

A Once Gorgeous Ruin

The point about Ayutthaya is that what you are looking at is merely the stump of a previously gorgeous assembly. Whereas now you see brick, before you would have seen gold. What remains is what the looting and pillaging Burmese didn't think worth removing. The rough inner structures whose dull surfaces are now returning slowly to nature under the humid skies were once coated with all the dazzling richness with which the Thais have always invested their temples and palaces. Only when you picture this can you imagine the former sumptuous splendor of the place. In the long official name for Bangkok is included the title "the new Ayutthaya". Ayutthaya of old would have resembled the lavish glory of the Grand Palace in Bangkok today, but on an incomparably greater scale.

And, as in Sukhothai, what the Burmese didn't take the museums have made off with. Most of the best pieces are in Bangkok, but the small **Chao Sam Phraya National Museum** contains some items. It's situated opposite the city walls on Rojana Road and is open every day except Mondays and Tuesdays.

For the site as a whole, notable features are **Wat Phra Sri Sanphet** within the former Royal Palace compound, the riverside **Wat Panan Choeng**, **Wat Phra Maha That** and **Wat Na Pramane**. It's charming to see that many of the great Buddha images are still venerated with flowers and offerings by the few remaining local inhabitants. Once these images were coated with gold which the Burmese had to melt off with the aid of fires — a procedure in which both nations were no doubt well practised.

In marked contrast to the rest of the site is the modern **Mong Kol Bo Phit** temple. It contains a large black bronze Buddha image, and its glittering exterior provides a reminder of the brilliant color harmonies that would have characterized Ayutthaya of old.

Bang Pa-In

Almost everyone visits Ayutthaya on a day-trip from Bangkok, and almost everyone includes **Bang Pa-In** in the excursion.

Fourteen kilometers (9 miles) from Ayutthaya, the former country residence and love-nest of Thai kings and princes is a strange and evocative mixture of Oriental styles and nineteenth century European influences.

Bang Pa-In resembles some of the garden-buildings at Versailles, though it's arguably more beautiful. There's an Observation Tower that looks as if it should be in a novel by Thomas Love Peacock, and classical statues in Carrara marble that are wholly and unashamedly European.

But nowadays a slightly forlorn elegance characterizes the place. The Chinese palace, the towers and ornate bridges built for joy still stand in their spacious setting among lawns and waterways but their glory is beginning to fade. Topiary elephants decorate the scene, but elsewhere the paint is peeling, the shutters are all closed, and the tiles have acquired a patina of mould. Love has departed from these places especially built for it

and it's as if they are resentful and in a sulk, refusing to put on their make-up any more.

Excursion by River

A good way to get to Ayutthaya and Bang Pa-In is on the combined bus/river-boat-excursion organized by the Oriental Hotel. You leave at 8 am, arriving back at

5 pm, and you can choose whether you go by coach and return by boat or vice-versa.

At 740 baht for the round trip it isn't cheap, but the buffet lunch aboard the boat, the Oriental Queen, is superb. The vast array of first-class food is the main reason for taking the coach first — this way you can relax after your meal on the four-hour river trip back. Done the other way round, you eat rather too

The Chao Phraya River at Ayutthaya, with Wat Chai Wattanaram. The ancient capital was surrounded by water for defensive purposes, and today the ruins appear attractive from water-level. Once glittering with gold and mosaic ornament, they were protected by a wall rising from the "moat".

early and then have a long afternoon of sight-seeing in front of you at the hottest time of day.

The highlight of the river trip in either direction during the dry season is the spectacular sight of the colony of open-billed storks at **Wat Pai Lom**, half way along the river. At first you catch sight of some isolated birds circling in the sky high above the river — then suddenly you are upon them and they are everywhere, hundreds, perhaps thousands of them, in

KANCHANABURI AND THE RIVER KWAI BRIDGE

A hundred and thirty kilometers (81 miles) west of Bangkok, Kanchanaburi makes a popular day-trip out from the capital. It's actually the main town of an attractive and almost wholly unspoilt province that repays a longer stay.

The road from Bangkok is a fast modern highway all the way. The only interest on

the sky and in the trees on the bank surrounding the monastery. These beautiful creatures migrate from India in September and remain here until May, or even later if the onset of the Thai rainy season is delayed. No-one knows how long they have been coming to this site but they are protected by the monks at the *wat* as sacred creatures.

You can also easily get to Ayutthaya from Bangkok by train. It's very cheap and the trip takes an hour and a quarter. There are numerous trains in each direction daily. When you arrive at Ayutthaya, mini-buses will take you to any of the sites in the area, including Bang Pa-In .

the journey is the town of **Nakhorn Phathom** half way along the route. Its famous **Phra Phathom Chedi** rises above the town and can be seen from the road on your right. It's the highest Buddhist monument in the world (127 meters) and marks the place where it is thought Buddhism was first taught in what is now Thailand. Clad in its brown tiles, it looks like a celestial hand-bell, waiting for a heavenly hand to reach down and clang it to mark the end of afternoon school. It was built in 1860 by King Mongkut (Rama IV) and contains inside it the smaller sixth century *chedi* that preceded it, a replica of which stands to the south.

The River Kwai Bridge

Kanchanaburi is first and foremost famous for the nearby **"Bridge over the River Kwai"**, and the museum and cemeteries associated with the construction of the war-time railway.

The infamous iron bridge is situated at the north end of the town. It is black and squat and, in the event, rather small. That such a structure could have been so crucial to the outcome of a global war seems inconceivable forty years on.

It was part of the railway built by the Japanese to supply their army in Burma. This overland supply route from the east became urgently necessary when the Allies gained control of the sea routes to Burma during the latter part of the war. Most of the line ran through jungle and rolling hills and was therefore impossible to make out from the air, but the bridge was clearly visible and so was the route's weakest point. The Allies made several attempts to bomb it, and finally, on February 13, 1945, they succeeded, using American planes based at Pandaveswar in India. The bridge was eventually reconstructed for post-war use — only the curved spans in the middle are part of the original structure.

The single track across it is still in use by trains running from Bangkok up to Nam Tok — you cross the bridge shortly after Kanchanaburi station. In addition people walk, cycle, and ride their motorbikes across it by means of planks laid end-to-end between the rails. It presents a colorful, even a picturesque little scene, the perfect picture of everyday Thai provincial life.

Between the bridge and the center of town is the **Kanchanaburi War Cemetery**, on your left coming back from the bridge. Almost seven thousand prisoners of war who died while working on the railway are buried here — mostly Dutch, British and Australian.

Jeath Museum

Close to the center of town is the **Jeath** Museum which displays information about the war-time railway in a reconstructed prison hut from the period.

As you enter the small compound on the banks of the river, a notice informs you that the name "Jeath" was used because "Death" sounded too horrific, and it was decided instead to take the initials of the nations whose prisoners largely built the railway, namely Japan, England, Australia, Thailand and Holland.

In a long bamboo hut, a replica of the type used in the camps, are displays of photographs and paintings of life on the "Death Railway". There's little else there — just a few objects such as boots, knives and tin plates. The photographs are for the most part less than horrific — in some the men even look quite cheerful. The paintings are more disturbing. Possibly excessive hatred guided the artist's brush. But the statistics bear out the most bitter depictions. Sixteen thousand prisoners of war are thought to have died, roughly 38 for every kilometer of railway built. The deaths, among local laborers, however, were much higher. As many as 200,000 may have died on the 415 km (257 miles) of track. The camp at the Kwai bridge was only one of 42 along the length of the line.

The museum is maintained by the temple, **Wat Chaichunphon**, which stands next to it.

Over the River

If you go along the road that runs by the river from the right hand side of the museum, after half a kilometer you will come to a small ferry. Between the museum and the ferry are some floating restaurants; one of these is the moderately-priced **Luan Poi**, ((034) 511897.

The infamous bridge over the River Kwai at Kanchanaburi. Built with materials brought from Indonesia, at immense cost in human lives, the central section was destroyed by Allied action in 1945. The new section (pictured here) allows the bridge to be used to this day, by pedestrians, cyclists and the trains of Thai railways.

The ferry takes you over the river for two baht. There, the road leads away to the left the three kilometers (two miles) to the **Chungkai War Cemetery**. It's 1,750 graves are immaculately kept. The track to the left of the cemetery leads down to the river.

Both of these Kanchanaburi cemeteries are run by the Commonwealth War Graves Commission and they contain the remains, almost exclusively, of prisoners of European descent. Most of the Asians

who died on the railway have no such memorial.

A Slightly Special Cave

Two kilometers (one and a quarter miles) further on is **Khao Poon Cave**. It's one of the nicer Thai caves, with a lot to see for very little effort. It is lit throughout by green, pink and white neon strips, and you are led by arrows along a winding passage with Buddhas, one reclining, the other cross-legged, at each end. The limestone formations are good, too, especially in and around the last cave. Entrance is by donation, and the whole establishment is run by some jokey young monks;

their pop music rises from behind the Buddha images out in the courtyard as you leave.

Further Afield

Fifty and Seventy-two kilometers (32 and 45 miles) respectively from Kanchanaburi are the **Bor-Ploy Sapphire Mines** and the **Erawan Waterfall and National Park**. Full details are available at TAT. But these are rather far for a one-day trip. Should you want to stay in Kanchanaburi in order to explore the area, try the **Kwai Yai Garden Resort** (reservations in Bangkok, (251-5223; 26 rooms; rates: moderate) where accommodation is in floating, reed-roofed raft houses.

Tourist Information

Kanchanaburi Province is considered worthy of a **TAT Office**. It's right where the buses from Bangkok stop on the main street, and the phone number is ((034) 511200.

Death and life beside the River Kwai. ABOVE: one of the graves kept up by the Commonwealth War Graves Commission; OPPOSITE: floating restaurants on the river on the Kanchanaburi side. The town, and the district as a whole, makes a very restful retreat from the noise and pollution of Bangkok.

Pattaya
and the
East
Coast
Resorts

CHONBURI

The stretch of coast from Bangkok to the Cambodian border is essentially the capital's playground. Though only developed in the last couple of decades, it has successfully taken over from the longer-established places to the southwest where the nearest resort, Cha-am, is a three hours' drive away. Pattaya, by contrast, is a mere two, and Bang Saen — which really is Bangkok by the sea — is just an hour and a half.

After Pattaya comes Rayong, and the popular but very small island of Koh Samet. Beyond this, the coast is still largely untouched by tourism.

Chonburi is a large town of no particular interest apart from its three temples. These are **Wat Dhamanimita** with its giant golden Buddha, **Wat Yai Intharam** with its multiple Buddhas, all facing you like imperturbable judges in a nightmare, and the tranquil **Wat Sam Yot**, looking out serenely over the coast.

Chonburi hosts street **buffalo races** every autumn, "on the 14th day of the waxing moon in the 11th lunar month". Contact TAT in Bangkok or Pattaya for details expressed in Western terms.

BANG SAEN

Ten kilometers (six miles) from Chonburi, and 100 km (61 miles) from Bangkok, is **Bang Saen**. Pattaya was developed with foreigners in mind, but Bang Saen is almost exclusively Thai. It's where hard-driven Bangkokians, with perhaps only one day's holiday a month and little spare cash, go with their children to enjoy themselves. The kilometer-long sandy beach is naturally very crowded at weekends, but its deck-chairs, showers, inflated tire inner-tubes and food stalls are exceptionally inexpensive.

Big Buddha at Pattaya. The modern statue occupies a spectacular site overlooking the coast above Jomtien Beach.

It's primarily a day-trip resort, but there is some reasonable accommodation available at the **Bangsaen Beach Resort** (℄ (038) 376675-7; 129 rooms; rates: moderate; reservations in Bangkok, ℄ 2533956), and the **Bangsaen Villa** (℄ (038) 377088; 70 rooms; rates: moderate; reservations in Bangkok, ℄ 2534380-1).

At the north end of the beach at **Sam Muk** fishing village there's a community of wild monkeys by a local shrine, with fine views from the cliffs out to sea.

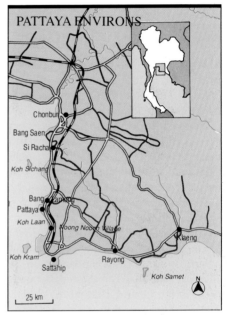

PATTAYA ENVIRONS

Chonburi
Bang Saen
Si Racha
Koh Sichang
Bang Lamung
Pattaya
Koh Laan
Noong Nooch Village
Klaeng
Koh Kram
Sattahip
Rayong
Koh Samet
N
25 km

And at Sinakarinwirot University's Bang Saen campus there's a **Marine Aquarium** with 43 tanks. Opening hours: 8:30 am to 4:00 pm (closed Mondays). Admittance 40 baht.

Seven kilometers (4.3 miles) from the beach there's the 18-hole international championship standard **Bangphra golf course**, with accommodation and a clubhouse.

A FREE-RANGE ZOO

Further inland, 11 km (seven miles) from the golf course, is the **Khao Kheo Open Zoo**, operated by the Dusit Zoo in Bangkok. Fifty species roam freely over a

490 hectare (1,200 acre) area, and you drive round catching sight of the animals as they wander in semi-liberty. There's also Thailand's biggest aviary here, an entire hillside enclosed with netting that even covers full-sized trees. You walk around inside the net along a perimeter path and count the exotic tropical species as they flit about all round you. There's accommodation in rest-houses set on a cliff — phone the zoo in Bangkok on (281 0000 for details.

SI RACHA AND KOH SICHANG

Si Racha is a small commercial port between Bang Saen and Pattaya. It's also the embarkation point for the island so loved by former Thai kings, Koh Sichang.

Si Racha is too busy to have developed as a tourist resort, but there is a most picturesque Thai-Chinese Buddhist temple situated on a small island, **Koh Lor**, connected to the mainland by a causeway. It's a classic place to take a *samlor* out to to see the sunrise.

There is also a choice of hotels in the town, all right on the waterfront and, indeed, in some cases built right out on stilts over the sea. The most elaborate of these is the **Grand Bungalow**, (((038) 312537; 13 rooms; rates: moderate; reservations in Bangkok, (392 1159). Among the others are the functional but delightful **Samchai**, (((038) 311134; 60 rooms; rates: inexpensive), the **Sri Wattana**, ((311307; 24 rooms; rates: inexpensive) and the **Si Wichai**, (((038) 311212; 38 rooms; rates: inexpensive).

For food — sea food is the speciality — try the good but rather expensive **Chua Lee**, or one of the garden-restaurants on the road out to Pattaya.

Boats to **Koh Sichang** leave every two hours from 7 am, except for the last boat of the day which leaves at 4:30 pm. The trip takes just under an hour.

The island has a town in its center, with a Thai temple at one end, and a Chinese one

raised high up at the other. Here are also the partially overgrown remains of a **Summer Palace** built by King Chulalongkorn. Begun in 1889, the palace was eventually abandoned by the king after the unpleasant experience of seeing the island occupied by the French in 1893 as they pressured the Thais into granting them territory neighboring on Cambodia. The ploy succeeded, and the shame and sorrow led to the abandonment of the royal residence.

Koh Sichang has some attractive beaches, among them **Haad Tawang**, close to the palace, and **Haad Tampang**. There's also the **Chakrapong Cave** with a chimney-like way up to the summit of a hill commanding a fine view over the island. Simple accommodation is available at the **Tew Pai Guesthouse**; either book in here or check carefully the time of the last ferry back to Si Racha — it's usually no later than the middle of the afternoon.

PATTAYA

SIN CITY

It's 2 am in the morning and in the warm night air a sun-tanned and totally naked Westerner is standing waving a beer can in the middle of the road. He's surrounded by a small crowd which includes a fully-dressed Thai girl who's clutching her handbag and pleading with him. A few feet away waves break softly on the sand, and down the road two policemen are approaching on white motorbikes.

Is it a comedy or a scandal? Your judgment of this scene will no doubt anticipate your opinion of **Pattaya** (pronounced by the Thais with the stress on the last syllable — Pat-ty-*ya*), Thailand's most outrageous and blatantly commercial (and Westernized) seaside resort.

Pattaya's potential was first realized in the sixties by a group of luxury yachtsmen, but with the coming of the Vietnam War and the establishment of a large American base nearby, it was fast transformed into a wild and raucous R & R facility. When the Americans left, the sex-tourists moved in to fill the vacuum.

As it exists now, Pattaya is the ultimate test of the traditional Thai virtues of spontaneity and ingenuousness. It's good to be able to report that for the most part the population comes out with flying colors.

Perhaps one of the reasons for this is that so many of the people working here come from Esarn, the despised agricultural region of the northeast. Much of the vigor,

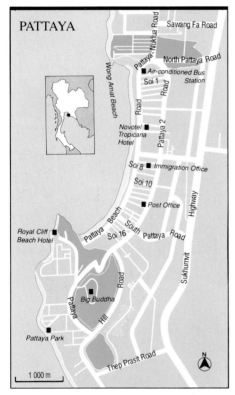

PATTAYA

good humor and occasional impulsive generosity of Pattaya people is rooted in this hinterland where rice farming, water-buffalo-tending and periodic drought are such hard masters.

Not that the place is without its problems. One of these is water. Pattaya has exceeded over and over again estimates made a few years ago of its probable fresh water requirement today. What is certain is that unless the height of the dam at Mab Prachan reservoir is increased soon, the

town will, in bad years and maybe even eventually in good ones, be faced with a problem for which there is quite simply no solution.

But the glittering, brash seaside town carries on, smaller than you'd expect, and almost entirely patronized by foreigners. A significant proportion actually live here, either running bars or simply retired, unable or unwilling to give up the easy life and the on-hand pleasures. The result is it's the most Westernized place in all Thailand.

GETTING THERE

Air-conditioned buses for Pattaya leave Bangkok from the Eastern Bus Terminal (Ekamai) every half hour (fare: 50 baht) until mid-evening. Bangkok hotels prefer to book their guests onto private buses — which may only be 10-seaters — at a cost of around 120 baht; these leave three times a day, roughly at 9 am, noon and 4 pm but in reality when all the passengers from the different hotels have been ferried through the traffic to the central departure point.

If you're going from Bangkok International airport direct to Pattaya you might be lucky enough to touch down at a time close to when one of the direct Don Muang — Pattaya mini-buses leaves. It's worth enquiring before taking the "limousine" into Bangkok. Airport-bound minibuses in the other direction can be booked at the **Air-conditioned Bus Station** (meaning the bus station for air-conditioned buses) on the first *soi* at the north end of Pattaya Beach Road.

A BIRD'S EYE VIEW

The buses from Bangkok leave the highway and enter Pattaya down the North Pattaya Road. North of here, between the Pattaya–Naklua Road and the sea, is an area that used to be quiet and rather exclusive but is currently being energetically developed. The main beach is **Wong Amat**. Pattaya proper extends for about 3 km

(2 miles), from North Pattaya Road along the whole length of the bay to where the land begins to rise to the headland. The busiest part of the town lies between the road running along the sea front, Pattaya Beach Road, and the first road parallel to it inland, Pattaya 2 Road. Connecting these two roads are no fewer than 31 side streets; some are numbered (Soi 1 to 16), others named, and some nameless. Traffic circulates anti-clockwise on a one-way system, running from north to south along Pattaya Beach Road, and than back again the other way along Pattaya 2 Road.

This district, then, the down-town area facing out onto the bay, is divided into North and South. The distinction isn't exact, but North, extending approximately down to Soi Post Office, is Pattaya without the pavement bars, souvenirs and disco music. It's not discreet exactly, but the hotels stand back from the road in their own grounds, and the restaurants and bars appear intermittently, rather than as a continuous frontage.

South of this the real nightlife sector begins. After a few blocks the main road sweeps inland along South Pattaya Road, leaving the final section of the beach strip, now with clubs, shops and bars on both sides, mainly to pedestrians.

Behind all this is the Thai town. Try taking a look at **Watchaimongkol Market**, open daily until 7 pm, on the right of South Pattaya Road (keep straight on where the mini-buses turn right to go up the hill towards Jomtien).

WATER SPORTS

The main beach at Pattaya is, unfortunately, now too polluted for swimming to be without risks. Water sports still keep going, but if you feel like a dip you really

At Pattaya you can find just about everything you require, and at any hour of the day or night. Brash and (to some) offensive, it's a seaside town designed to please unattached males first, and anyone else who turns up second.

should hop on a mini-bus and go over to Jomtien.

You can expect to pay the following prices for beach sports on Pattaya Beach: Water scooters — 200 baht per hour; Water-skiing — 800 baht per hour; Speed boats — 800 baht per hour; Para-sailing — 200 baht for a five minute flight.

AFTER DARK

Pattaya's nightlife in every way rivals you as you pass, Pattaya's *raison d'etre* advertises itself all too effectively. But the resort does have *some* other attractions after sunset.

Tiffany's, ((038) 429642, was the original transvestite show in Pattaya. Thai film director Pisan Addaraserani made a feature film *Raktoraman* ("Tormented Love") based round the show, and using many of the cast, in 1987. It's still going strong, three times a night, seven days a week, as is the nearby **Alcazar Cabaret**,

Bangkok's — many prefer it on account of the more relaxed ambiance. But there's the same range, and indeed, when the US Navy's in town, many of the same faces as well.

Discretion isn't a characteristic of Pattaya, and to walk down the southern end of Beach Road after around mid-afternoon is to see on very open display the world's so-called oldest profession. With open-fronted bars whose girls wave and call to

It's a difficult job to catch sight of a girl on-stage in Pattaya. Almost all the many shows there are put on by transvestite males. Cross-dressing has a long tradition in southeast Asia, but in Thailand it has become a national speciality.

((038) 429746, now housed in a big new auditorium. Both shows are exceptionally — perhaps a touch too — professional, and the entrance fee includes a free drink.

In the Pattaya Resort Hotel is the very popular **Disco Duck**, complete with the nowadays standard video-screens.

The **Marine Bar** is vast, and as just one of its attractions shows films nightly on a full-sized cinema screen; you watch them from your table. It's open to the sea at the side and any breezes that are around help the fans with the ventilation. There's also a boxing ring, and upstairs there's the **Marine Disco**.

Enthusiasts for Japanese **karaoke** can find it at the **Sarabu Cafe**, next to the Snow White Cafe on the right of the Pattaya–Naklua Road.

WHERE TO STAY

The **Royal Cliff Beach Resort** ₵ (038) 421421-30; 727 rooms; rates: expensive; reservations in Bangkok ₵ 282 0999; telex: CLIFFEX 85907 TH) is situated high on the headland separating Pattaya and Jomtien, poised to make the best of Pattaya whichever way it develops.

Its large number of rooms and suites in no way implies mass tourism — instead, they are sub-divided into family suites with two bedrooms, "honeymoon" suites right down near the sea, and the ultra-luxury suites in the new Royal Wing (with its own private beach). The Royal Cliff is one of the great hotels. It has facilities for a huge range of sports, its tennis courts are "all weather", and it even has special boats for use by guests on its two private beaches.

The **Novotel Tropicana** (₵ (038) 428-645-8; 186 rooms; rates: average and above; reservations in Bangkok ₵ 236-2891; telex: 85910 NOVO TH) was one of the first luxury hotels in town, and its central position continues to give it a certain distinction.

The **Montien** (₵ (038) 419155-6; 320 rooms; rates: average and above; reservations in Bangkok ₵ 233 7060; telex: 85906 TH) and the **Royal Garden Resort** (₵ (038) 428122; 142 rooms; rates: average and above; reservations in Bangkok ₵ 252-4638; telex: 84437 ROPAT TH) are both central and on Beach Road.

The classiest accommodation at Wong Amat is at the **Wong Amat Hotel** (₵ (038) 428118-20; 207 rooms; rates: average and above; reservations in Bangkok ₵ 2784375-6; telex: 87172 WONGBKK TH).

You won't find in Pattaya the ultra-cheap accommodation available in so much of Thailand. But attractive rooms for 200 to 300 baht aren't difficult to find

(except when the US Navy's in town). The area around Soi Post Office is the place to start looking.

RESTAURANTS

Krua Suthep, ₵ (038) 422722, on Pattaya 2 Road, opposite the Alcazar Cabaret, serves fine traditional Thai food in an elegant setting. Excellent and moderately priced Thai food is also available at **Somsak,** ₵ (038) 428987, at the Pattaya 2 Road end of Soi 4. Meanwhile **Dolf Riks,** ₵ (038) 428269, on Soi 1 serves highly acclaimed Dutch and Indonesian, as well as international-style, dishes.

For Thai food served as a circus act in the manner of Phitsanulok province, hurry round to the **Flying Vegetable** on Pattaya 2 Road. Meals, flung in a wide arc from the frying-pan, are invariably caught on a plate by an imperturbable waiter some distance away, to the cheers of attendant coach-parties.

There are plenty of restaurants catering for Moslem visitors — one of them is **Al-Sheikh,** ₵ (038) 429421, on South Pattaya Road which serves vegetarian and non-vegetarian foods in the Pakistani style.

The **Green Bottle Pub** (₵ (038) 429-675) serves European and Thai food in an English setting to the accompaniment of a 3-piece band, and the prize-winning **Rim Talay Restaurant** on Soi Chaiyapruek offers fresh sea-food cooked in Thai style.

A SOUVENIR PORTRAIT

In the same way that the Thais excel in counterfeit clothes and recordings, so, too, are they as painters adept at producing accurate imitations of the work of the great masters. If you want to impress your friends by exhibiting one of Rembrandt's most illustrious masterpieces in your living-room, Pattaya's the place to come in search of it. They'll even substitute your profile for that of the original sitter if you can let them have a photo for a couple of hours.

Prices are low, and the artists very skilful. They can paint a straightforward portrait of you, of course, almost with their eyes closed. The **Siam Art Shop, (** (038) 429045, in South Pattaya is one of several places where you can watch them at work.

GETTING AROUND TOWN

Transport in Pattaya is by converted pick-up vans. Red and white stickers inside the vehicles state the fares: En route maximum 5 baht; charter: two persons — 30 baht per trip; each additional person 5 baht per person. In many cases these figures have been scratched out — one wonders who by.

You can also get taken where you want to go by motorbike. Groups of youths wait with their machines at major intersections, and you hire them out like taxis. You say where you want to go, they name a fare and off you go.

Renting a motorbike is exceptionally popular and outlets are everywhere. **Jenny Hotel, (** (038) 429645, is one good place, but there are many more. Expect to pay about 150 baht per day for a Honda Dream, more for the bigger machines.

JOMTIEN BEACH

This runs south from Pattaya after the headland on which the Royal Cliff Hotel stands. The road from Pattaya arrives at the coast and then turns left. Jomtien Beach extends for about a kilometer to the right and for many kilometers leftwards along the road.

The beach is busiest on the stretch to the right. For about half its length there are continuous beach umbrellas and deck-chairs, every 20 m (66 ft) or so under the eye of a different food and drink establishment. When the color of the deck-chair frames changes, you know you're in a new territory. There's no charge for the deck-chairs, but you are naturally expected to order something — prices are everywhere very reasonable. Beach-mats are provided free if you ask.

To the left, arrangements continue at first in the same manner. Then gradually the umbrellas peter out until, after a couple of kilometers, the new cafes stand empty (at least in mid-week), the wind hisses through the grass, girls with nothing to do go through each other's hair looking for lice — or grey hairs — and the rare van lumbers over the pot-holed road. Occasionally someone bumps past on a water-scooter, but otherwise the blue sea breaks undisturbed on an empty shore.

Soon all this will be changed as building is going on apace, but for the moment this far end of Jomtien is very much a betwixt-and-between world.

Back under the brilliantly-colored umbrellas, Jomtien is Pattaya without some of the hassles. But these things are relative. Para-sailing, windsurfing and speedboats are all here — indeed, Jomtien is something of a windsurfer's Mecca. But for the discos and the high-pressure salesmanship of the night-life, then you must go back to Pattaya. In this respect, at least, it's quieter this side of the headland.

New hotels are going up at Jomtien every year, as well as tower-blocks of condominiums. The **Jomtien Hill Resort** (((038) 422378; fax: 422378; 64 rooms) has average-and-above price rooms. The **Marine Beach Resort** (((038) 231129; 65 rooms), the **Sea Breeze** (((038) 425651; 80 rooms) and the **Surf House International** (((038) 231025-6; 55 rooms) all offer accommodation at moderate rates.

And at the far end southern of the beach the gigantic **Ambassador Resort Jomtien** (((038) 231501-40; fax: 231731; rates: average and above; reservations in Bangkok (2540444) has an astonishing 2,500 rooms and, not surprisingly, elaborate conference facilities.

Mini-buses run over to Jomtien from Pattaya but you have to negotiate the price. Thirty baht is about normal. Coming

Hire a jeep? Enjoy the Big Splash at a private park? Go waterskiing? Parasailing? Rent a condominium apartment, or even buy one to retire to? Or just lie on the beach – it's all possible at Pattaya.

back you can sometimes get a ride for 20 baht as the vehicles quickly fill up with passengers all going more or less the same way.

PATTAYA PARK AND BIG BUDDHA

On the road from Pattaya to Jomtien, a side road leads off on the right for **Pattaya Park**. Here there's a fresh-water swimming pool complex next to the sea featuring its famous **giant slides**. It's open from 8:30 am to 6 pm. Admission to the slides and pool is 50 baht, 30 baht for children "under 120 cm" (4 ft). The park is part of the Pattaya Beach Resort.

High on a hilltop above Jomtien, with a road all the way up, stands the **Big Buddha**, its vast white torso wound round with a yellow scarf. Day-of-the-week Buddhas stand round the forecourt. The park's proximity to Pattaya is apparent in signs asking people not to climb up onto the images. Above the main Buddha's head a red light warns off low-flying aircraft.

With 24-hour access, it's a good place to visit at night. The food stalls are vacated, the tropical moon shines on the statues, and the breeze flutters the scarves, making the images seem to stir in their meditations.

The shrine was completed in 1977 and its official name is Buddha Vanothayan, or Khaoprayai. There's a good view of the coast from the approach road.

TOURIST INFORMATION

There are two free "what's on" magazines published in English that give an up-date on restaurants, hotels, night-life and the like in the resort. They are *Explore Pattaya* and *Pattaya Tourist Guide*. The *Sun Advertiser* is very useful if you're interested in buying property in the town. All should be available at TAT and in hotel lobbies.

In addition, TAT maintains a helpful office at 382 Pattaya Beach Road, ((038) 428750.

Communications and Visa Renewal

The **Post Office** is, unsurprisingly, on Soi Post Office. For international direct dialing (IDD) phone-calls, go to the **Pattaya City Telecommunications Center** on South Pattaya Road, 800 m (half a mile) from Waatchaimongkol Market.

The **Immigration Office** (for renewing visas) is on Soi 8, ((038) 429409.

AROUND PATTAYA

On the other side of the Sukhumvit Highway (the main road from Bangkok) there are a number of attractions, all situated down the Phra Pracha Nimit Road.

Three kilometers (two miles) from the highway is **Pattaya Elephant Village** where 12 elephants go on show daily at 2:30 pm (bookable through agents). The keepers and their beautiful animals are all from Surin, where the annual Elephant Round-Up is held (see OFF THE BEATEN TRACK section). It's a congenial place, with one or two very young animals usually on show. They're not averse to taking you round at other times of day too, but then a tip — perhaps 30 baht — is in order.

Finally, the **Siam Country Club**, (((038) 428002; enquiries in Bangkok (215 0900 Ext 162), offers a high-class 18-hole golf course, plus billiards, and accommodation in 30 rooms.

MINI SIAM

Back on the main road, at the intersection with North Pattaya Road, is **Mini Siam**, where miniature versions of Thailand's best known sites are on display for an entrance fee of 200 baht (100 baht for children). There's a new **Cultural Center** on the same site.

NONGNOOCH

Twenty kilometers (13 miles) to the east of Pattaya there's **Nong Nooch Village**, ((038) 429372-3. It's similar to Bangkok's

Rose Garden. Large numbers of coach parties arrive daily to see elephant parades, traditional dances from all over Thailand, and other shows, all in a spacious 400 hectare (900 acre) garden setting featuring waterfalls and orchids.

NAKLUA

In **Naklua**, three kilometers (two miles) north of Pattaya beyond Wong Amat (see above), you are suddenly back in Thailand. Wooden fishermen's houses on stilts, piles of garbage, and colored scarves round sacred trees bring you back to the realities of conditions elsewhere in the country.

KOH LAAN (CORAL ISLAND)

One hour (fare: 40 baht) from Pattaya by public ferry, this off-shore island is underdeveloped after the mainland, but it's no unspoilt paradise. The beaches are on the west side, i.e. the far side when coming from Pattaya, and the main beach is **Tavan**.

Tavan's front is entirely occupied by restaurants and souvenir stalls. The two-tier ferries from Pattaya cannot come right inshore so passengers are taken to the beach in long-tail boats. Some crazies even cross over from Pattaya on water-scooters — what happens if the engine fails doesn't bear thinking about.

Very few visitors stay on Koh Laan — almost the entire trade is of people coming over for the day. Consequently, Tavan Beach is really another alternative beach to Pattaya's, like Jomtien down the coast on the mainland.

The scene at midday is of a bay filled with the gaily-colored wooden ferries, long inshore craft, plus a bevy of water-scooters and touts for water-ski takers. Para-sailers take off and land at a platform moored out in the bay. Then, at precisely 3 pm, the entire beach population — almost all consisting of organized groups, Koreans, Kuwaitis, Germans — can be seen making for the long boats, as if news had just broken of some impending global catastrophe. By 3:30 pm the beach is deserted, and the cafe women are busy washing up while the men count the day's takings.

There are other beaches on Koh Laan besides Tavan. **Tong Lang** has a couple of cafes, each with its handful of faded beach umbrellas, while **Tion Beach** is a boat-trip (or a difficult walk) on the other side of Tavan. Both are very much quieter than Tavan.

Other and far less frequented off-shore islands are **Koh Sak**, **Koh Pai** and **Koh Khrok**. Individual deals must be done with Pattaya boatmen to arrange transport.

RAYONG AND KOH SAKET

East of Pattaya is **Rayong**, 185 km (115 miles) from Bangkok by Highway 36.

It's an ordinary Thai country town with little to see that can't be seen elsewhere. It's best known for its *nam pla,* a garlic sauce popular with Thais.

If you have half an hour to spare, you might spend it taking a look at the 12 m (39 ft) reclining Buddha in **Wat Pa Prandu**, leaning on his left side rather than the traditional right.

Six kilometers (four miles) from the town, going back in the direction of Pattaya, is **Hat Sai Thong**, a sandy beach from which boats will take you to the nearby island of **Koh Saket**. The crossing takes twenty minutes. It's a small island, but there's accommodation available at **Ko Saket Phet** (25 rooms; rates: moderate; reservations in Bangkok (271 2750).

The coastline immediately after Rayong has recently seen a spate of development and now boasts a number of fine resort hotels, plus some others.

On the grandest scale, standing at the end of a secluded wooded peninsular, is the **Rayong Resort** ((211 0855; 167 rooms; rates: average and above; reservations in Bangkok (255 2392 and fax 255 2391).

Just as nice, though, and with a better beach, is the **Novotel Rim Pae Rayong** telephone and fax (℃ (038) 614678; 109 rooms; rates: average and above; reservations in Bangkok ℃ 246 9491; fax 246 9974), some 10 km (six miles) further along the coast.

Close to the Novotel are the comfortable **Palmeraie** (℃ (01) 211 7763; 65 rooms; rates: average and above; reservations in Bangkok ℃ 213 1162 and fax 213 1163) and the much less sophisticated **Ban Phe Resort** (118 rooms; rates:moderate; reservations in Bangkok ℃ 250 0928). Back towards Ban Phe, the **Ban Phe Cabana** (℃ (01)211 4888; 33 roms; rates: average and above; reservations in Bangkok ℃ 280-1820 and fax 280 3648) occupies a less-than-satisfactory situation, while in Ban Phe itself the **Pines Beach Hotel** (℃ (01) 321 0885; 150 rooms; rates: moderate) is an excellent, modern hostelry.

KOH SAMET

This attractive and popular holiday island is nowadays crowded with small hotels, all relatively inexpensive and all of the beach-bungalow type. There are only a handful of rooms with air-conditioning, and there is an increasingly serious water shortage in the latter part of every dry season (April and May). But if what you want is a simple, relaxed holiday, yet with plenty of others like yourself around, Koh Samet could well provide the answer.

A company called **Sea Horse** operates minibuses from Bangkok, but it's an expensive, cramped and often time-consuming service — far better to take the public air-conditioned bus from Bangkok's Eastern Bus Station (Ekamai) on Sukumvit Road to **Ban Phe**, the small port 200 km (125 miles) away from which the boats to the island depart. The new road, Highway 36, by-passes Rayong and allows the journey to be done in under three hours. The fare is 70 baht, and buses leave hourly from 5 am to 10 pm.

The crossing from Ban Phe is six and a half kilometres (four miles) and takes half an hour. The boats are colorfully painted, wooden, and accommodate around 50 people. There is no timetable and craft leave when it's judged there are enough passengers to make a profitable journey. The fare is 20 baht, though more is asked if there are only a few of you and you're impatient to be off.

ARRIVING AT NADAAN

The scene at the simple wooden jetty where you arrive is like something out of the eastern novels of Joseph Conrad. The ham-

let — known as **Nadaan** — is merely a cluster of grass-roofed huts in a clearing in the trees. Boats moor alongside each other and it is necessary to clamber across the adjacent decks to reach the jetty. The few simple restaurants and food stalls will not detain you, and mini-buses wait to take you the short distance to the long line of sandy beaches on the other side of the island.

If your destination is the first, and in many ways best, beach, **Hat Sai Kaeo**, it's actually just as easy to walk. Follow the broad sandy road past the **Health Center** on your left, and in five minutes you will be at the gate into the **National Park** where an entrance fee of 5 baht is exacted. The office of the National Park is here too but has no information to offer other than a small duplicated map which doesn't contain the names of the hotels.

The mini-buses turn right, but if, at the sandy cross-roads immediately past the National Park entrance, you continue straight ahead you will almost at once find yourself by the sea, half way along Hat Sai Kaeo beach.

Passengers on the mini-bus should note it first reaches the coast at **Ao Phai** beach, and then continues south, turning inland to

Koh Samet's unpretensious beach restaurants and bungalows are ideal for a simple, relaxed holiday by the sea.

skirt a rocky outcrop, until it arrives at **Ao Wongduan**. After Ao Wongduan the road is effectively for pedestrians only. The fare almost anywhere on this mini-bus is ten baht.

If your destination is Wongduan — or Ao Cho — you can take the boat all the way, though this will take you longer than if you get off at Nadaan and take the bus. Only boats wholly filled with Wongduan-bound passengers go directly there without stopping at Nadaan first.

WHERE TO STAY

Accommodation on Koh Samet is all relatively simple, ranging from two-room bungalows with air-conditioning in the evenings renting out at around 600 baht a day to very basic huts, containing little more than a mattress and a mosquito net, for as little as 50 baht. All prices go up at

The colors of the ocean — ABOVE: dried fish being prepared the natural way; OPPOSITE: untangling nets on the Gulf of Siam. Thai fishermen decorate the prows of their boats as a matter of course, always in the most devastatingly vivid colors.

weekends and during public holidays, and all are negotiable if you plan a stay of more than a few days.

Koh Samet is a very different place midweek and at weekends. It is common not to be able to find a room on a Saturday night — this is when the island fills up with Thais from Bangkok seeking a well-earned rest. They frequently come in large groups, and on arrival set up in the shade of the palm trees (Thais have a horror of darkening their skin with sunlight) and, opening the first bottle of Mekong of the trip, prepare to serenade the rising moon with the latest chart successes. Some of the classier places claim to vet locals arriving in large groups with the aim of excluding raucous elements "and gigolos". But most visitors will agree they provide welcome relief from the rows of *farangs* reading novels and perfecting their sun-tans.

At the time of writing, electricity is generated privately and is rarely available before sunset or after midnight.

SAI KAEW

Beginning at Sai Kaew beach in the north, **Diamond** (℃ (01) 321 0814; rates: inexpensive) has an ever-increasing number of bungalows, and a restaurant offering very friendly service and reasonable food. It's a successful family establishment in a prime position at the top end of the island's best beach. The swimming is excellent, and if you feel like being alone you can walk round onto the rocks of the nearby headland and gaze at the expanse of blue sea and the islands to the east.

A short way down the beach, **Toy** (℃ (01) 321 0975; rates: inexpensive) has only a few bungalows, but boasts an excellent restaurant that attracts many visitors from neighboring establishments. **Sai Kaew Villas**, (℃ (01) 321 0975; rates: moderate) offers good quality bungalows and cocktails. **White Sand** (rates: inexpensive) is large and with a good restaurant. The last place on this beach is **Sun Sand**, close to the concrete mermaid that separates Hat Sai

Kaew from Ao Phai beach. It's very cheap, and a popular late-night partying venue.

AO PHAI

The top end of this beach is dominated by **Naga** (rates: inexpensive), an inspired establishment where Mozart flute concertos accompany breakfast and there is a good library of Western books. It's situated on a rocky hillside, and flowering plants frame the view so that you can imagine you are in Capri. The 20 bungalows are elegant but basic, but the food is excellent and served in large portions. Not surprisingly, it tends to get crowded at dinnertime. Naga is perhaps most celebrated for its cakes and varieties of bread, all made on the premises daily to the exacting standards of the English owner.

Next door is **Nui's** (rates: inexpensive), a smaller place with ten bungalows and excellent ice-cream. Lastly on this bay is **Ao Phai Inn** or **Nop's Kitchen** (((01) 2112968; rates: inexpensive) a shady but slightly dusty place with a large number of bungalows.

Continuing south, you arrive next at **Sea Breeze** (((01) 321 0975; rates: inexpensive), a straightforward place with thirty bungalows. Very inexpensive accommodation can be found at **Tub Tong**, while **Samet Villas** (rates: inexpensive) has a mere eight bungalows, each with fans and shower.

Ao Phai beach is divided into several coves, and the last of these contains **Pudsa Beach** (rates: inexpensive) with 23 bungalows, and **Tub Tim** (rates: inexpensive), a friendly establishment attractively situated behind palm trees and with a small cocktail bar.

AO CHO

The coastal footpath now rises to cross a rocky section — when it descends again you're at **Ao Cho**. This is a tranquil little bay with exceptionally clear water and a small wooden jetty where the boats of the "White Shark" line depart for Ban Phe four or five times a day. Here, **Tantawan** (((01) 321-0682; rates: inexpensive) serves simple local

dishes in an idyllic setting. After fried fish and rice and a bottle of Kloster, you feel you could stay here for ever. Further accommodation is available at a very slightly higher price at the next place, **Tarn Tawon**.

WONGDUAN

A minute's walk takes you over to the next bay. You are now approaching Koh Samet's up-market sector, but the first place, **Samet Resort** (rates: inexpensive)

is unassuming. The **Malibu Garden Resort**, however (rates: moderate; 30 rooms; for reservations (Pattaya (038) 423180) marks the beginning of the **Wongduan** group of establishments catering for a clientele interested in mini-golf (on a concrete course), *petanque* and a Saturday night discotheque. All these delights are to be had at **Wongduan Villa** (((01) 321 0789/-211 0509; in Bangkok (03) 5250220; rates: moderate). The **Wongduan Resort** ((01-3210731; rates: moderate; reservations from Bangkok (2500423/4/5/6) offers quiet, large bungalows, while **Sea Horse** (70 rooms; rates: inexpensive) has a large number of less ostentatious places.

Whether Wongduan is really worth the extra cost depends on your tastes. But most people will find it preferable to the beaches further south.

A VIEWING POINT

After Wongduan the beaches become rockier and the accommodation rather rough and ready. More bungalows, however, are going up all the time, and given that there is little room for development further north, this area is bound to change in character before very long.

Immediately before Bungalow Lung Dam a sign "Sunset 200 m" points to the right, and a narrow path leads up into the trees. The island here is very narrow, and this is an excellent place to cross over to its largely uninhabited west side.

Once across, you arrive at a viewing point of great beauty. Before you is a vast expanse of ocean, dotted with fishing boats with their arms outstretched. To the right lie the hills of the mainland, beautifully arranged as an attendant vista. Ban Phe is clearly visible. The rocks of this inhospitable side of the island slope away below you. It's a wonderful place at any time of day, and an easy walk from Wongduan to see the sunset.

AO PHRAO

There is one bay on the west side of the island, **Ao Phrao** ("Paradise Beach"). It's quiet, backed by wooded cliffs and, of course, it faces the sunset. Ferries will take you there direct from Ban Phe for a minimum of 100 baht. Otherwise boats go from Nadaan, or you can walk (15 minutes) from Sea Breeze bungalows. Vehicles can't go the whole way as the sand road becomes a steep and rocky track for the last 200 m.

There are three bungalow establishments at Ao Phrao. **S.K.Hut** (22 rooms; rates: inexpensive) is at the south end by the wooden jetty. Next comes **Dhom** (☏ (01) 3210786; 17 rooms; rates: inexpensive), probably the best bet of the

three. And last there is the rather basic **Ratana's** (10 rooms; rates: inexpensive).

Ao Phrao is probably too quiet for most people. There is coral at the jetty end, said to be the best on Koh Samet, though there are better examples round the outlying islets. Coral generally, though, doesn't compare with that in the clearer Andaman Sea off Thailand's southwest coast.

Note: Malaria is present on Koh Samet and visitors should be sure they are taking the necessary precautions.

CHANTABURI

Two hundred and eighty kilometers (174 miles) from Bangkok by Highway 36, this town is famous as a center for the mining and cutting of gems. Sapphires and rubies are found nearby and you can buy them in this town as cheaply as you'll find them anywhere.

Chantaburi's other claim to fame is Thailand's biggest Roman Catholic Church, the **Church of the Immaculate Conception**. It was built by Catholic refugees from Vietnam between 1905 and 1909.

Outside town is the **Khao Sar Bab National Park**. Its **Pliew Waterfall** is a popular local beauty spot, and mini-buses leave for there from outside Chantaburi's Municipal Market. Reasonable accommodation is provided at the **Hotel Eastern** (℄ (039) 312218-20; 142 rooms; rates: moderate).

TRAT PROVINCE

Close up against the Cambodian border, this is the easternmost part of Thailand. It

from just before Klong Son but should not be attempted after dark. Total walking time is around an hour and a quarter. Klong Son itself is a peaceful fishing village with a clean and reliable guest-house, the **Mannee**. The boat crosses back to the mainland in the early morning.

The smaller islands are currently being actively developed — TAT in Bangkok or Pattaya should be able to provide you with up-to-date details.

Trat is an attractive small town. Simple

contains several virtually untouched islands, including the large **Koh Chang**.

Boats to Koh Chang, as well as to **Koh Koot**, **Koh Kradat** and **Koh Rad**, leave from **Laem Ngob** cape, 20 km (12 miles) south of Trat town.

For respectable accommodation on Koh Chang there's the **Bangbao Beach Resort** (℄ (039) 511597). For inexpensive and basic huts, but with a reliable restaurant, try the **Diamond Beach Resort** on Head Sai Khao. To reach the latter you must take the daily boat from Laem Ngob to Ao Sapo Rot (departs around lunch-time) and from there walk, via Klong Son, over the mountain to the beach. The path is signposted

but good accommodation is available at the **Hotel Muang Trat** (℄ (039 511091; 123 rooms; rates: inexpensive), overlooking the night market. Western food is served in the Coffee Shop.

Lastly, note that the islands are malarial; make sure you're taking prophylactic tablets while — and after — visiting the region. See under HEALTH in TRAVELERS' TIPS section for details.

Monks on a beach on the Gulf of Siam. All Thai boys enter a monastery for a time during adolescence, and even in adult life often return for periods of retreat. Being a monk is in no way necessarily an 'all-or-nothing', life-time calling in Thailand. OVERLEAF: a Thai truck makes for the end of the road.

The
South
and
Phuket

HUA HIN

Hua Hin is Thailand's traditional royal resort, and its life-line has always been the railway.

Nowadays the country's main north-south road runs right through the middle of the town, but in the 1920's it was the construction of the single-track railway down from Bangkok that first put Hua Hin on the map.

At last the wealthy could escape the suffocating heat of the capital in April and in three hours be in their villas along the sands, cooled by the breezes off the Gulf of Siam. Foreigners arrived to inspect the exotic new resort, and Hua Hin became the Nice of Asia. People played golf — that newly fashionable game popularized in Asia by the young heir to the English throne — on a picturesque and intriguing **18-hole golf course** opposite the quaint wooden station, rode horses along the sand, and socialized in the celebrated Hua Hin Railway Hotel.

Elsewhere in the world Railway Hotels tend to be rather down-market affairs catering for commercial travelers who arrive late and have to be away on the first train of the morning. Not so Hua Hin's. In its hey-day this colonial-style hotel on the sea was every bit the equal of the Oriental in Bangkok and the Raffles in Singapore.

Then, as suddenly as it had come, fashion abandoned Hua Hin. Created by the railway, it was killed by the road — the road east from Bangkok, to Bang Saen and Pattaya. For twenty years from the mid-sixties, Hua Hin's charms came to seem decidedly frowzy.

WHERE TO STAY

Nowadays, however, things are looking up. The Railway Hotel, not so long ago a place with only a handful of spider-filled rooms from which to watch the few remaining horses sheltering from the sun beneath faded beach-umbrellas, has been

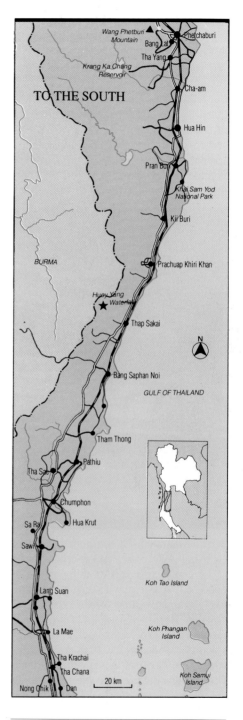

Fishing boats at Hua Hin. Attractive old-world wooden buildings cluster round the harbour — many of them have been converted into restaurants offering the freshest possible sea-food. It's a busy area at night in an otherwise quiet town.

extensively and beautifully renovated by the French Sofitel company. Re-named the **Sofitel Central** (℡ (032) 511012 or 511015; 207 rooms; rates: expensive; booking in Bangkok on ℡ 2330256; fax: 511014), it has retained all the style of its past while installing the comforts and conveniences of the modern era. Afternoon tea is now served in the old lobby, a period jazz band serenades you at cocktail time, and soon vintage cars will transport you the short distance from the station. The topiary gar-

den and its much-photographed elephant (with painted wooden tusks) remains.

Of course this sort of thing is not to everybody's taste, and if you prefer a more lively ambiance then there is the **Royal Garden Resort** (℡ (032) 511881/4; 220 rooms; rates: expensive; booking in Bangkok on ℡ 2516859 or 2524638 or 2528252; telex: 78309 ROGAHUA TH) with its Jungle Disco half a kilometer to the south down the beach.

The hotel Sofitel Central, Hua Hin. This famous hostelry used to be known as the Railway Hotel and saw in its heyday much high living. It was renovated and considerably enlarged in 1987.

For more or less budget accommodation, the **Jed Pee Nong Hotel** (℡ (032) 512381; 35 rooms; rates: moderate) on Damneonkasem Road is very popular — clean and good value.

RESTAURANTS

Many fine sea food restaurants are to be found by the Harbour. Of these, the **Mee-karuna Restaurant**, ℡ 511932; rates: moderate, and the **Saeng Thai Restaurant**, ℡ 512144; rates: moderate, are especially recommended.

A small way from the center of town is the **Bann Tappikaew**, 7 Naebkhehat; ℡ 512210, a very attractive restaurant based round a beautiful wooden house. Most of the tables are in the garden which fronts onto the sea. It's very popular with the better-off local Thais, and the cuisine is classical Thai.

Foreign food isn't hard to find in Hua Hin either. Close to the station, the **Friendship Restaurant**, ℡ 511373; rates: moderate, specializes in steaks, to the accompaniment of distant and rather plaintive vocalists; German food can be found at the **Thai-German Restaurant**, 22/32 Petchkasem Road, ℡ 512536; rates: moderate; and the **Sailom Hotel**, ℡ 511890/1; rates: average and above, offers Japanese food as well as Thai.

Further Information

Many of the facilities you're likely to need in Hua Hin are concentrated in the broad road running directly down to the beach from the station, Damneonkasem Road. The **Tourist Information Service Center**, ℡ (032) 512120, is there, as is the **Post Office**, and a clutch of tourist-oriented restaurants, souvenir stalls, tour agents, together with a variety of budget — and other — hotels.

The **Bus Station** isn't far away from this complex, though in fact there is no station as such — buses wait at the four corners of a large cross-roads, where Descharnuchit Road crosses Srasong Road. It's a 10 minute walk, or a 10 baht pedi-cab ride, from the station.

AFTER DARK

Everything in Hua Hin has the appearance of being prosperous and even up-to-date. Even the **Night Market**, in many places attractive because of its very sleaziness, is here clean and brightly-lit. It's adjacent to the Bus Station.

But a more attractive place to go at night, and a colorful place at any time, is the **Harbor**. Here, old wooden houses

Access to the beach for the rest of us is by Damneonkasem Road, running direct from the station and passing the Sofitel Central on the right.

Where this road reaches the sea there are some rocks, but for the rest the beach is sand and, according to the authorities, safe for children. North of this point is the harbor, then, a kilometer further on, the royal **Summer Palace**, situated on the sea, with formal steps leading down onto the sand.

back onto the water, and many of them have been made into restaurants. As you might expect, sea food is their speciality (see under RESTAURANTS, above).

THE BEACH

Hua Hin's long sandy beach extends both north and south of the harbor. There is no road running along the front — instead, large houses, a few hotels and one palace back directly onto the shore. Commercial development along the shore-line is as a result almost entirely non-existent, and the exclusive quiet sought by the original visitors is effectively maintained.

It is possible to walk right past the palace for most of the year, and this is the best place to get a glimpse of the buildings — relatively modern and set in spacious grounds. (There is an access lane from the main road through Hua Hin, but from there you can see comparatively little.) When members of the royal family are in residence, however, sentries seal off this portion of the beach. His Majesty prefers to wind-surf — a sport which he is said to enjoy particularly — in peace.

Hua Hin. Up-market development has meant the beach is very quiet, with private villas backing directly onto the extensive sands.

KHAO TAKIAB

South of Damneonkasem Road the beach sweeps uninterrupted to **Khao Takiab** ("Chopstick Hills"), four kilometers away. If walking in the heat seems too hard, you can get a bus from the Bus Station — they leave every half hour and the trip takes fifteen minutes.

Khao Takiab is a rocky outcrop on the sea's edge. There's a tall white Buddha close to sea-level, a monastery higher up, and various shrines and outhouses sited in scenic positions. The monastery's regimen appears relaxed. Monkeys live in the trees in the first part you come to, and food for them — bananas and peanuts — is on sale at the entrance. They won't bother you if they see you haven't bought anything.

Eight kilometers (five miles) further south is **Khao Tao** hill with its twin peaks, and the very quiet **Suan Son** beach backed by pine trees. Fishermen will also take you from here (or from Khao Takiab) to the off-shore island of **Sing Toh**.

PHETCHABURI

Sixty kilometers (37 miles) to the north of Hua Hin, is easily accessible by road or rail. Approaching the town by either means you can see its two main attractions, a palace and a temple, perched on their twin hilltops ahead of you.

Rama IV's Summer Palace, and the **Museum** inside it, are open from 9 am to 4 pm Wednesday to Sunday (closed Monday and Tuesday). To get there you have to walk from the town center, up a once-paved road that was clearly meant for horse-drawn traffic. Now it's broken, and if you don't fancy walking in the heat, you'll have to wait for a chance motorbike — of which there are usually plenty — to give you a lift. The palace features an observatory — astronomy was one of old King Mongkut's enthusiasms — and you get an excellent view from the top.

You can easily walk from the Summer Palace across the col to **Wat Tra Keow**, five minutes away on the neighboring hilltop. This has just been extensively renovated and is now a sparkling jewel in a magnificent location.

The large *chedi* that you pass on the way there is at the time of writing in a dilapidated condition, but it's interesting to go inside it, and to come out via some steps onto a ledge at a higher level.

From the temple you can go down to the road without going back to the Palace, by a track leading through monastery buildings.

Phetchaburi is rich in temples, and **Wat Khao Bandai It** with its leaning *stupa* (said to show the original patron's preference for one of his two wives), together with **Wat Yai** and the several other *wats* close to it in the center of the town, are all well worth a visit.

A Buddha Cave

Khao Luang Cave is two kilometers (one and a quarter miles) out of town and contains an underground shrine. A mini-bus will take you there for 20 baht, will require the same again to bring you back, and may ask for something more for waiting for you.

You arrive at a little group of wooden houses and the cave entrance is 50 yards ahead up a paved track. There is a padlocked gate across the entrance and it is very much a matter of chance whether or not there will be someone there to unlock it and accompany you down.

OTHER TRIPS FROM HUA HIN

Cha-am

Hua Hin's less than regal sister resort is nothing more than a four kilometer (two and a half miles) long sandy beach backed with casuarina trees along which, over the

Roof decoration at Phetchaburi. The small country town was a favorite of King Mongkut (Rama IV) and is rich in temples, both up on the hill overlooking the town and down in the central area near the railway station.

years, a variety of hotels and guest-houses have established themselves. Whereas Hua Hin is dominated by its palace, colonial-style hotel and second homes of the very rich, Cha-am is pleasantly democratic and easy-going. Few Westerners stay there, but it's very popular with Thais.

Cha-am gets very full at weekends as it is one of the closest resorts to Bangkok, but on weekdays, even in high season, you can have the beach almost to yourself. It's a pleasant, unassuming place unspoilt by

passes within a kilometer of the beach, and if you arrive by bus you'll be put down where motorbikes are waiting to transport you to the sea (fare: 5 baht again).

Small restaurants and hotels extend for about a kilometer both to the left and right of the point where you arrive on the front. There are many budget and near-budget places, and one five-star place, the **Regent Cha-am Beach Hotel** (((032) 471-493/9; 420 rooms; rates: expensive; bookable in Bangkok (251 0305; telex 72217 REGCHAM

the international invasion that is the bane of so many other resorts in Thailand.

Getting to Cha-am is no problem. It's on the railway, slightly disguised as Ban Chaam, and on the country's main north-south road. Most foreigners visit Cha-am, if at all, as a side-trip from Hua Hin, and from here too you can take either the train or a bus. Going by road is probably easier as there are plenty of buses, at least until 6 pm, after which there are none at all. The fare is 5 baht. The main road from Bangkok to the south

Sign at Khao Yai National Park. Thailand's National Parks are excellently kept up, and this is the country's oldest, containing a number of animals notably elephants.

TH). And poised to compete with it in the up-market stakes is the **Dusit Resort and Polo Club** (contact the Dusit Thani Hotel in Bangkok for further information). There are in addition several other more or less grand establishments along the beach between Cha-am and Hua Hin.

Pa La-u

This waterfall lies 63 km (39 miles) inland, near the Burmese border. It's a series of cascades in jungle settings, and there are Karen villages and a reservoir nearby. If you don't have your own transport, the only feasible way to get there is by taking a day trip. Public transport is timetabled for the benefit of the local villagers, and buses consequently leave the up-country areas early in the morning and return from Hua Hin in the afternoon. This is the reverse of what the tourist requires, so unless you plan to spend several days there — in which case you'll need a guide as well as a great deal of mosquito repellent — you have little choice but to pay your 600 baht and join an organized tour. All the agents in Hua Hin run these, but according to demand, not every day.

KHAO SAM ROI YOD NATIONAL PARK

As you drive south from Hua Hin, after passing extensive pineapple plantations (recognizable by the bluish sheen of the leaves of the cactus-like plant) you come to the small market town of **Pranburi**. There is nothing to detain you here, but as you continue south an extraordinary spectacle begins to appear on the horizon to the left. The turrets and pinnacles you are seeing are the summits of the sheer limestone hills known as Khao Sam Roi Yod ("300 peaks"), and the National Park that has been created

around them is one of the most attractive places for naturalists in all Thailand.

Without a hired car, transport into the Park used to be difficult. Now, however, there is a minibus service between Pranburi's town center and the Park Headquarters. You'll have to ask your hotel staff for the times of this new service, and they may conceivably be reluctant to give them to you as most hotels in Hua Hin run their own private tours (in conjunction with a local agent) when demand is sufficient. Public bus services to Pranburi from Hua Hin Bus Station are frequent during daylight hours.

A WILDLIFE PARADISE

The Park consists of spectacular limestone hills that rise sheer out of salt and semi-salt marshes. The marshes form the habitat for numerous bird species, and this is the best of the Thai National Parks for observing waders. Other birds to be seen here are herons, blue crab-eaters, bee-eaters, egrets, white-breasted kingfishers and white-bellied sea-eagles. Most of these birds are migratory and spend the summer in China, Siberia or Northern Europe — the best time to see them here is between November and January.

For the most part the birds occupy the saltwater and semi-saltwater mud-flats. Up on the hills are found serow (a form of goat-like antelope whose habitat is inaccessible crags), porcupines, crab-eating and dusky leaf-eating monkeys, and the very rare, cat-like fish tiger.

The 98 km (61 miles) square Park isn't without its problems. Much of the mud-flat area is outside its jurisdiction and prawn-farming has become popular with the local fishermen. This involves increasing the amount of sea-water in the creeks, but the increased salinity is killing the mangrove trees, home to the insects that bring the birds to the area. The Park authorities are responding by planting new mangroves in areas under their control, but the basic conflict of interests persists.

UNCROWDED PLEASURES

The National Park in general has many attractions, but most notable are its rugged interior and its caves.

Phraya Nakhon Cave is the most popular. It's situated 500 m (1/3 mile) from **Haad Laem Sala Beach**, and as it's a long, rough trek from Bang Pu (the nearest village), most people get there by boat. Its oddest and most striking feature is that it contains a royal pavilion, put there to receive King Rama V in 1896. This is currently about to be redecorated and will doubtless make a striking spectacle, lit by the shafts of sunshine that strike the cave floor from two large holes in the cave roof.

Kaeo Cave is also close to Bang Pu and is noted for its brilliant white limestone formations (*kaeo* means "shining" in Thai). A guide is essential as the cave has hidden ledges that are very dangerous.

Sai in Thai means "ficus", and these trees surround **Sai Cave**'s wide opening. It's a 15 minute walk up from the beach — there are steps all the way but it's steepish. The entrance is 300 m (980 ft) above sea level. Check on the beach that there's someone up at the cave to operate the lamps (the fee for the lamps and guide is 30 baht). It's an averagely interesting limestone cave, but with no special features.

Pine-backed **Sam Phraya Beach** is a short drive from Headquarters (on the coast in the far south of the Park). You can camp there, and there is one food and drink stall. You can also stay at Haad Laem Sala Beach (see above) where there are four bungalows; there are another four at Headquarters.

The best way to see the interior of the park on a short visit is to take a boat trip up the creek. At 150 baht per boatload per hour, this is excellent value, and the views of the high pinnacles, which fall sheer down to the river in places, are spectacular. For these trips, enquire at Headquarters, or at Khao Daeng Village. Early morning and late afternoon are the best times to see wildlife, as well as for taking photos.

KOH SAMUI ISLAND

There is nothing really worth seeing in **Surat Thani** (885 km (549 miles) from Bangkok; domestic airport; mainline rail link), though there is an interesting monastery, Wat Suanmoke, in the forest close to the nearby town of **Chaiya**. Most people head straight on for **Koh Samui**, a rather large, hilly island 35 km (22 miles) from the mainland south of Surat Thani.

Koh Samui has been a popular tourist destination since the late 1960's when it was "discovered" by the hippies. Now everyone is getting in on the act, and quite classy beach hotels and restaurants have begun to appear. The present situation is that the more popular beaches have a wide range of facilities, while the less frequented places still retain something of their earlier, drug-culture atmosphere.

Forest and rice-fields together make up a huge proportion of the country's inland scenery. The forests vary little from season to season, but the paddy fields change dramatically from wet season to dry. OPPOSITE: two views of the central Thai forest in Khao Yai National Park; ABOVE: rice fields after the monsoon.

GETTING THERE

You can fly direct from Bangkok's Don Muang airport with Bangkok Airways. They depart six times a day and the round-trip fare is 3,900 baht. Ferries run to Samui from Surat Thani and from **Donsak**, an hour's drive to the south. Boats leave Donsak at 8 am, 9:30 am, 3 pm and 5 pm; the trip lasts one and a half hours, and the fare is 40 baht. For the slightly longer (two

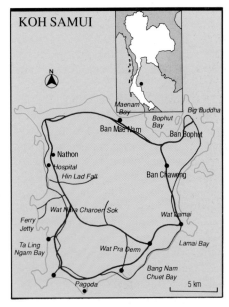

KOH SAMUI

hour) trip from Surat Thani boats depart at 7:30 am, midday and 2:30 pm in the dry season (November to May) and at 7:30 am and 1:30 pm only during the rainy season (June to October). The fare is 60 baht.

NATHON

All ferries arrive at **Nathon**, the only town on the island. It's a busy little place with a Post Office, an Immigration Office, a Catholic Church (masses on Sundays at 8:30 am and weekdays at 6:30 pm) and travel agents.

The attractions of Koh Samui are its large size, its pastoral quiet and its very extensive sandy beaches. The interior is hilly, and though modern facilities are now available in many places, it's never hard to be on your own.

The biggest of these is the semi-official **Songserm Travel Center,** ((077) 421228/-421078/421316-9, just to the left of the pier; **Paradise Seagull Tours** a few doors further on can also be recommended.

A BIRD'S EYE VIEW

But nobody stays in Nathon. Transport on Samui is well-developed, with a modern concrete road extending round the 58 km (36 miles) of the island's periphery. Buses leave in droves from first light till sunset for the beaches on the north and east sides of the island (fare 15 baht), and even after dark they can be privately hired as "taxis", but at a much higher rate, for the thirty minute trip.

Essentially, there are two "big" beaches, Chaweng and Lamai. More isolated clusters of bungalows are sited south of these, and this southern strip is where the cheapest accommodation can be found. North of Chaweng and Lamai, on the beaches of **Maenam** and **Bophut**, the situation is somewhere between the two, and some very attractive places, neither too developed nor too remote, can be found on this north coast of the island. For Bophut beach, take a bus that advertises its destination as "Big Buddha".

Some agents will try to interest you in bungalows they are in contact with while you are still on the boat crossing over from the mainland. They will probably tell you the island is overrun with tourists and finding a room is difficult. This will almost certainly not be the case — recent newspaper reports have suggested that Samui has over-anticipated demand for accommodation by as much as 40 percent. Besides, agents can only book you into places they can contact by telephone, and many beach hotels in Samui aren't on the phone.

An outstandingly informative map, showing all the hotels and clusters of beach huts, is the *Guide Map of Koh Samui, Koh Pha-Ngan and Koh Tao,* usually on sale on the ferries for 35 baht. Nowhere else in Thailand has such a detailed tourist map.

CHAWENG BEACH

The island's premier strip is **Chaweng Beach**, and it really is very beautiful, coconuts palms leaning out over white sand, and a coral reef off-shore. The beach slopes gradually, so quite a lot of sand — more than at Lamai — is exposed at low tide. Chaweng extends for 3 km (2 miles), with Chaweng Noi, ("Little Chaweng") adding another kilometer to the south.

Walking the length of the beach, the island's recent history is laid out before you. At several points fishermen sit under the coconut palms, watching their boats and waiting for the evening's fishing. They are the original Samui. Elsewhere are low-price bungalows offering "magic mushroom soup", representing the first influx of Westerners who disturbed the primordial quiet of the island. Then there are the up-market establishments with striped deckchairs and advertisements for cocktails. These represent the yuppies, the latest arrivals.

The nicest part of Chaweng Beach is the quiet north end, where friendly and unassuming, and in some cases even rather chic, clusters of bungalows overlook the islet known as **Koh Matlang** (or Mudlung). Here the **Matlang Resort** ((077) 421063; 27 rooms; rates: moderate) is smartish and has a garden, yet is very reasonable. Moving south, **Moon Bungalows** (12 rooms; rates: inexpensive) is relaxed and charming. **O.P. Bungalow** (20 rooms; rates: moderate) is notably clean and specializes in Chinese food.

After an undeveloped gap you come to the **Samui Cabana** (40 rooms; rates: moderate), an impressive place with sophisticated food and drinks. Close by is the friendly if basic **Montien** (12 rooms; rates: inexpensive). The **J.R.** ((077) 421402; 20 rooms; rates: inexpensive) offers a range of accommodation and pleasant service.

In the central and southern stretches of the beach several establishments attempt to go up-market. Notable among these are the **Chaweng Cabana** (℄ (077) 421377/9; 26 rooms; rates: average and above) and, especially, the **Pansea** (℄ 272-222 Ext 187; 30 rooms; rates: expensive; reservations in Bangkok ℄ 2356075-6; telex: 87654 WOLDWID TH). But the natural conditions on the beach are so idyllic it's difficult to see what else, over and above what everyone offers, is really needed.

This tendency to go up-market reaches its peak at the southern end of the beach where the buses from Nathon first hit the coast. Here the **First Bungalow** (℄ (077) 423444; 60 rooms; rates: moderate), is smart, has a shop and a pricey restaurant, while round the corner on Chaweng Noi the **Imperial Samui Hotel** (rates: expensive; reservations in Bangkok ℄254 0023 ext. Samui office, fax: 2533190) offers luxury accommodation.

LAMAI BEACH

Lamai faces south-east and is separated from Chaweng by a rocky headland where a couple of coves offer do-as-you-please seclusion. **Coral Cove Bungalows** (20 rooms, rates: inexpensive) is casual and friendly — ask the bus to put you down at the Brown Sugar "reggae" cafe.

Lamai basks in the tropical sun in sleepy languor, but its mass of coconut trees in fact hides an extensive network of sandy roads linking up not only numerous bungalow hotels but also some rather trendy ice-cream parlors, discotheques and bars. Even so, Lamai remains less developed than Chaweng, though the difference is unlikely to last long. If Chaweng's beach has the edge, Lamai's the place for laid-back indulgence and dreamy ease.

Fishing boats moor at Lamai's northern end, and the beach proper doesn't really begin until you've passed the little river and the sign announcing "Ban Lamai". At this northern end, **Rose Garden Bungalows** (℄ (077) 421410; 16 rooms; rates: moderate), has a quiet, half forgotten air that might appeal to some people.

You can take your pick of the bungalow hotels on the main stretch of the beach. They almost all fall into the inexpensive category, and in some of them you could easily imagine you'd taken a time-trip back twenty years. The **Lamai Inn Bungalows** (℄ 421427; 40 rooms; rates: inexpensive), is just one of many. Only the **Best Resort** (30 rooms; rates: moderate) aims to cater for a very slightly more affluent clientele.

At the south end of the beach, where the buses emerge from the sandy Lamai lanes onto the hard road, is **Cafe Roma** (rates: moderate) offering Italian food (including pizza), ice-cream and cocktails.

The **Nightlife** on Chaweng and Lamai consists of three discos, the **Flamingo** on Lamai, and the **Arabian** and **Madonna** at Chaweng.

TONGSAI, BOPHUT

Luxury rooms are available at the **Imperial Tongsai Bay Hotel and Cottages** (rates: expensive; reservations as for the Imperial Samui on Chaweng), while on **Bophut Beach,** the **Samui Palm Beach** (Telephone and fax: ℄ (077) 421358; 20 rooms; rates: average and above) is both comfortable and relaxed.

KOH PHA-NGAN ISLAND

All in all, Koh Samui is a back-packer's paradise that is very well patronized by those it aims to please and is beginning to look further afield. Simpler and more natural places than those on the main beaches can still be found, but if you're convinced that Samui is already just too popular for anyone seeking the true Blue Lagoon life, then you should head north for the second largest island in the group, **Koh Pha-Ngan**.

The ferry from Nathon to Koh Pha-Ngan leaves twice a day, at 10 am and 3 pm (returning from Pha-Ngan to Samui at 11:30 am and 4:30 pm). The 25 km (16 miles) trip takes 35 minutes, the fare is 45 baht.

The morning boat connects with the ferry from the mainland to Samui; it always waits for it, so you can be sure of making the trip from the mainland to Koh Pha-Ngan direct, without having to spend any time at all on Samui if that's what you want.

Boats also run to Koh Pha-Ngan from Bophut Beach. They're sturdy fishing boats with an enclosed section under the square superstructure and they carry around 20 people. They put you down at Haad Rin Beach. Departures are at 9:30 am and 3:30 pm; the return boats from Pha-Ngan leave at 9 am and 2:30 pm. The fare is 50 baht each way.

THONG SALA

Koh Pha-Ngan is a great contrast to Koh Samui. This is clear the moment you arrive at the harbor and one-street port, **Thong Sala**. Whereas in Nathon on Samui it's all travel agents booking trips to Bangkok, Kuala Lumpur and Singapore, in Thong Sala the typical shopkeeper is asleep under a straw hat, and his wares are medicines for humans, medicines for animals and sea shells.

A proportion of the visitors arriving on the morning boat immediately take the connecting fishing boat for Haad Rin, the island's most popular beach and inaccessible (except on foot) by land. A few opt to stay in town, perhaps at **Sea Surf Bungalows** (14 rooms; rates: inexpensive). Most, though, settle down to a welcome second breakfast in one of the three simple cafes situated where the road reaches the beach, and then make off by mini-bus "taxi" or newly rented motorbike for one of the bungalow establishments along the island's southern coast between Thong Sala and Baan Khaay.

SOUTH COAST

The bus for Baan Khay (fare 15 baht) bumps over the sand road loaded with crates of soft drinks and tourists' rucksacks. Signs with names like "Liberty" and "Green Peace" point down narrow tracks to where the sea glitters blue between palm trees.

Each of these clutches of bungalows has a whole stretch of the long sandy beach to itself. Some, such as **Laemthong** (10 rooms; rates: inexpensive) are on rocky outcrops commanding extra-beautiful views, and rooms cost as little as one and two US dollars.

At **Baan Khay** the road ends, and as a result the places immediately after there do a good trade. The first of them, **Thong Yang** (14 rooms, rates: inexpensive), with some of its bungalows perched on rocks washed by the waves, is the nicest.

HAAD RIN

This is Koh Pha-Ngan's most popular beach. It lies at the far south-eastern corner, and is actually two beaches, one on either side of a narrow isthmus. It's a three-minute walk from one beach to the other.

The east-facing beach usually has some small waves, welcome to some people, but it's the west-facing one that has the nicer bungalows and restaurants. Of these, **Rin Beach Resort Kitchen and Bakery** does excellent cakes and is a pleasant place to sit and gaze at the sea from. By and large, though, Haad Rin is something of a betwixt-and-between place, aiming for a degree of sophistication but with none of the advantages — or the quality of beach — of the best places on Koh Samui.

WEST COAST

The west coast of the island is generally low-lying and life in its holiday bungalows is very quiet. Pines line the beach, crickets chirr in the night, birds twitter in the bright mornings. At **Laem Son** (10 rooms; rates: inexpensive) the food's good, though the beach isn't special. There are fishing boats and solitude. Further along, at **See Thanu** (12 rooms; rates inexpensive) the beach is better.

There are no metalled roads anywhere on the island, and virtually no electricity.

Much of the transport is by motorbike — riders will take you anywhere for roughly the same price as the buses (which may only run every couple of hours).

KOH TAO

There are many other islands in the Koh Samui group. An irregular service connects Thong Sala with **Koh Tao**, 47 km (29 miles) away to the north. The boat-owner will undertake the three hour trip on demand if there are enough people to make it worth his while; otherwise he goes about twice a week. The fare is 80 baht.

There are plenty of places to stay on Koh Tao. It's mainly known for an off-shore islet, Koh Nangyuan, where three beaches, each facing a different way, have become joined back-to-back. It's claimed to be a unique phenomenon.

A MARINE PARK

Very spectacular is the **Ang Thong National Marine Park**. This consists of 40 steep and forested islands 31 km (19 miles) west of Samui. They are uninhabited except for a National Park staff of 30 on Ta Lap ("Sleeping Cow Island"). There are simple bungalows to rent on this island, but almost everyone visits on day trips from Samui, and the Park authorities are no doubt happy to keep things this way.

Attractions are snorkeling, diving, and clambering up a steep track on **Mae Koh** ("Mother Island") to see a brilliantly green saltwater lake surrounded by cliffs called Talai Nai.

Tours from Samui are organized on Tuesdays, Fridays, Saturdays and Sundays by Highway Travel, (421290 or 421285. You leave at 8:30 am and are back for 5 pm (150 baht, lunch included). On Wednesdays, Saturdays and Sundays you can go with Samui Holiday Tours, (421043 or 421204, on the same terms.

Drying squid. The beauty of all but a few Thai seaside resorts is that normal fishing and farming life goes on side by side with modern tourism.

PHUKET

Over the last couple of decades Phuket has become Thailand's premier tourist destination. It has its own airport, and several foreign airlines, in addition to Thai International, have acquired rights to fly there direct. The road from Surat Thani across the isthmus to Phuket on the western coast (four and a half hours by minibus) passes through spectacular limestone mountains

on an excellent modern highway.

Phuket is big, 810 sq km (312 square miles), and actually hardly a true island at all — it's connected to the mainland by a causeway. It's hilly, and its name derives from the Malay word *bukit* meaning "mountain". It was an important and prosperous province long before the first foreigner thought of lying on any of its numerous beaches, and under-sea tin mining has always been important.

A BIRD'S EYE VIEW

Basically, it's the indented west coast that has all the finest beaches, while the lower-lying east coast is more involved with commerce and industry. Phuket Town, also often referred to simply as "Phuket", lies on the island's eastern side, two thirds of the way down from the causeway.

This means that tourist development has tended to be on the western beaches themselves, with the town remaining relatively untouched by the massive foreign influx.

From Promthep Cape in the south to the Sarasin Bridge in the north, then, Phuket's major beaches are Nai Harn, Kata Noi, Kata, Karon, Patong, Kamala, Surin, Bang Tao, Nai Yang and Mai Khao. Details of **accommodation** will be given on a beach-by-beach basis.

BEACH BY BEACH

Rawai

Before looking at these western beaches, mention must be made of **Rawai Beach,** east of Promthep Cape. Popular with local people, it has no up-market developments

and remains an unassuming place with good sea food—at, for instance, the **Salaloy Restaurant** ((381297; rates: inexpensive). Nearby there is a **gypsy settlement** similar to the one at Pang Nga. **Promthep Cape** itself is a classic place to go to see the sunset — at the weekend in the company of coachloads of other enthusiasts.

Close to Rawai is the **Phuket Island Resort** (((076) 381020; fax: 215956; 300 rooms; rates: average and above; reservations in Bangkok (252 5320-1), a large hotel attractively spread over a hillside sloping down to the sea and commanding superb views to the south. One of the many islands you can see, Koh Bon, is owned by the hotel, and during the daytime a boat

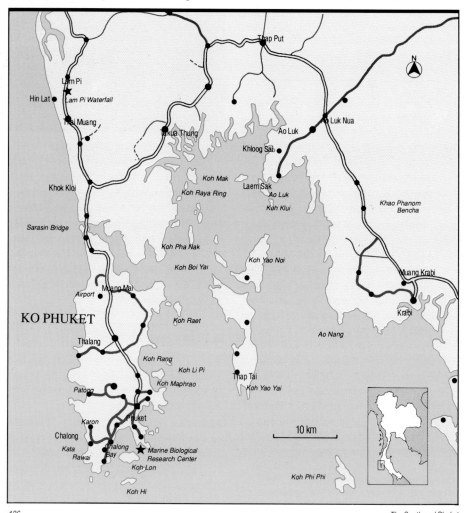

ferries hotel guests across to a private beach and barbeque restaurant.

This spacious hotel also features Thai, Japanese and European restaurants, a discotheque, and a wide variety of sports and sea-sports facilities.

Nai Harn

This beautiful beach is unspoilt and enclosed by well-wooded headlands. At the southern end stands one of the island's very best hotels, the **Phuket Yacht Club** (℄ (076) 214020-7; fax: 214028; 108 rooms; rates: expensive; reservations in Bangkok ℄ 251 4707).

Kata and Kata Noi

The coast road that connects Nai Harn and Kata affords the most spectacular view on the island at its summit. Looking north, Phuket's sequence of magnificent sandy beaches, each separated by a rocky headland, is spread out before you. The road arrives back at sea level at a point where Kata Beach lies to your right and Kata Noi ('Little Kata') to your left.

Kata Noi is dominated at the north end by the **Kata Thani Hotel** (℄ (076) 216632; 193 rooms; rates: average and above; reservations in Bangkok ℄ 214 4538; telex: 69516 KATHANI TH). Everywhere else is much more basic, but generally the fishermen's huts — some of which offer accommodation and food — are nowadays kept away from the actual beach front, at least at the showy north end.

Kata is a fine bay, a deep bite into the land with a picturesque island plumb in the middle. At the southern end is the comfortable **Kata Inn** (℄ (076) 214828-9; fax: 214828; 86 rooms; rates: average and above). Thailand's only **Club Med** (℄ (076) 214830-1; telex 69526 CLUBMED TH; 300 rooms; rates: expensive; reservations in Bangkok ℄ 253 9780) is also situated on this beach, very attractively built in traditional Thai styles and with the usual wide variety of facilities. The **Boat House Inn and Restaurant** (℄ (076) 215185; telex: 69532 YACHT TH; 36 rooms; rates: expensive)

offers genuine comfort and elegance without ostentation.

Karon

Between Kata and Karon are situated a number of shops selling souvenirs, a branch of the Thai Farmers' Bank, and several important diving centres (See DIVING, p.131).

Karon Beach itself is open, long, and has few trees. The beach is backed by low dunes behind which there's a brackish creek; behind this runs the road, and on

that, facing the sea, are the hotels.

Karon has only recently been developed and lacks the comfortable appearance of longer-established places. There are already many hotels, however. The **Phuket Arcadia Hotel** (℄ (076) 214812-6; fax: 321178; 255 rooms; rates: expensive) is large and modernistic, rising to 11 stories. The **Tavorn Palm Beach** (℄ (076) 214835-8; fax: 215554; 210 rooms; rates; expensive) is also modern and rises to four stories, while the **Phuket Island View** (℄ (076) 212696; 51 rooms; rates: average and above) offers accommodation in solid bungalows.

Karon to Patong

Take the new coast road connecting Karon

Phuket is Thailand's most highly developed resort with a wide variety of beaches down its long western shoreline. Every life-style is available, with the exception only of the very basic. Many possibilities for excursions of one day or longer — to Phang Nga, Phi-Phi or even the Similan Islands — completes the picture.

and Patong and on the way you will pass the **Meridien Phuket** (℃ (076) 321480-5; fax: 321479; 470 rooms; rates: expensive; reservations in Bangkok ℃ 2548147-50). Standing on its own bay, this is a deluxe establishment part-owned by Air France and specialising in, among other things, sports facilities. (See LASTLY page 191 for further comment).

Out on the headland south of Patong proper the **Coral Beach Hotel** (℃ (076) 321106-13; fax: 321114; 200 rooms; rates:

expensive; reservations in Bangkok ℃ 252-6118) is half a mile out of town and has its own small beach.

Patong
Patong Beach is everything opponents of mass tourism dislike and fear most. A vast coconut grove fills a basin of flat land backed by hills and fronting onto the sea, and not so very long ago all there was was a narrow road running parallel with the water and linking up a few idyllically-sited huts and a monastery. Today there are restaurants and shopping centers, hotels and bars, along the entire strip as well as some way inland; motorbikes roar off into the

morning and local girls call out at foreign men just as if they were in Hat Yai or Pattaya.

Patong in other words has become Phuket's fun center, young, slightly raucous, but with as yet none of Pattaya's air of polluted seediness. It had to happen somewhere, and if Patong can avoid Pattaya's mistakes it will probably remain for some time some people's number one choice.

Discos, bars and European-style restaurants aren't only found along the sea front. More of them line a recently-developed street in mock-European classical style running at right angles to the sea in the center of town, while to the north the castellated yet strangely anonymous **Paradise Complex** manages to be simultaneously reminiscent of Rotterdam and something out of Tolkien's *Lord of the Rings*.

Patong offers a big choice of places to stay. The **Club Andaman** (℃ (076) 321102; fax: 321527; 128 rooms; rates: average and above; reservations in Bangkok ℃ 270 1627), with its bungalow rooms set in spacious grounds, still survives, though nowadays increasingly hedged around by high-rise development, while the **Patong Beach** (℃ (076) 321 3016; telex 69521 PATONG TH; 122 rooms; rates: average and above; reservations in Bangkok ℃ 2330420) is a traditional hotel right in the center of town. The **Patong Merlin** (℃ (076) 321070-4; fax: 216429; 209 rooms; rates: average and above; reservations in Bangkok ℃ 2532641), the **Holiday Inn Phuket** (℃ (076) 321020; fax: 321435; 280 rooms; rates: average and above; reservations in Bangkok ℃ 234 0847) and the **Holiday Resort** (℃ (076) 321101; telex; 69540 HOLIDAY TH; 105 rooms; rates: moderate) are just three among the many other places offering international-standard accommodation.

Meanwhile, towering in pink and pale green over the Paradise Complex's 200 shops, cafes and a gay bar, stands the glitzy, brand new **Royal Paradise Hotel** (℃ (076) 321666-70; fax: 321565; 250 rooms; rates: expensive; reservations in Bangkok ℃ 260-3254-5) which, with its sunken poolside chin-level bar, pastel tapestries and general air of metropolitan chic, aims to be a pleasure complex in its own right.

You can eat in a wide variety of cuisines in Patong, Italian, German — and even Indian, at the **Shalimar** (℄ (01) 723 0488).

Kamala and Surin

North of Patong the coast road is currently only passable by adventurous motorcyclists prepared to get off and push in places. **Kamala** and **Surin** beaches are best

suites'; reservations in Bangkok ℄ 250-0746) would probably be more than happy to agree it is the most expensive place on the island.

Nai Yang

To reach **Nai Yang**, take the road to Phuket International Airport, but instead of entering the compound keep left, and you will come to the beach some 4 km (2.5 miles) further on, down a side road signposted **Nai Yang National Park**.

reached from Phuket Town — head north and turn left at the Heroine's Monument. Surin, with its rough waves, is magnificent to look at and has a **9-hole golf course**, but you *cannot* swim there as off-shore dredging in search of tin has created a lethal undertow.

Surin and Kamala are relatively undeveloped, but just to the north of Surin are two top-class hotels. The **Pansea** (℄ (076) 311249; fax: 311252; 76 rooms; rates: expensive) offers traditional-style but luxurious bungalows scattered over a steep slope running down to a private bay, while nearby the ultra-exclusive **Amanpuri** (℄ (076) 311394; fax: 311100; 40 'pavilion

The road arrives at the southern end of the long stretch of sand that extends north for a good 15 km (9 miles). The beach is for the most part deserted, and as such must rate as Phuket's nicest. What facilities there are are all at the southern tip, at the end of the access road. There's one hotel, the giant **Pearl Village**, (℄ (076) 311338; 163 rooms; rates: average and above; reservations in Bangkok ℄ 252 5245; telex 65539 VILLAGE

OPPOSITE: Islam begins to make itself felt in the south of the country: the Dubai Mosque, Phuket. ABOVE: The Pansea Hotel, Phuket. The hotel consists of luxury bungalows overlooking a private beach. The pattern is typical of many Thai beach-hotels.

TH) but it's set back slightly among palm trees and in no way dominates the beach.

For the rest, everything's very pleasantly relaxed and Thai. Indeed, the beach is so long that international tourism would find it difficult to make serious inroads into it; being part of a national park should help to protect it as well. At the south end there are deck-chairs and beach umbrellas, and you can even have rides on an elephant. But from there the sand extends northward into the haze, backed by casuarina trees — an ideal camping location.

And Nai Yang merges into **Mai Khao** (Airport Beach), the lonely extent of sand where between October and February the big sea turtles lumber ashore at night to lay and then bury their eggs.

Finally, if you take the road south of Nai Yang, you will eventually come to the small beach known as **Nai Thorn**. It's a really delightful ride over pastoral hills and through agricultural villages that could be a hundred miles away from Kata or Patong. Nai Thorn has fishing boats, but there's no accommodation available at the time of writing.

PHUKET TOWN

Not many people stay in the town, but it's an attractive enough place nevertheless, prosperous by Thai standards, with a touch of Portuguese influence in the architecture, some simple shops, and generally considered a nice place to work in or retire to.

Take a taxi up **Khao Rang** hill and you'll find a pleasant restaurant and cafe that catches the breezes off the sea and has a fine view over the town and surrounding country.

Transport inside the town is by little pick-up taxis, and the fare is a standard 10 baht. Transport out of town is by open-backed buses holding 20 or so passengers, also referred to as "taxis". These depart from outside the market in Jawaraj Road or, in the case of Rawai buses, from beside the roundabout a short distance away.

Phuket Town has a **Post Office** on Montri Road, an **Immigration Office** (for renewing visas) on Phuket Road, near the **Boxing Stadium**, and a **TAT Office**, ℭ (076) 212213 for a wide range of information and help.

Superior accommodation in Phuket Town can be found at the **Pearl Hotel** (ℭ 211044; 250 rooms; rates: average and above; reservations in Bangkok ℭ 260-1022-7; telex: 69510 PEARL TH), the **Metropole** (ℭ(076) 215050; fax: 215990) and at the **Phuket Merlin** (ℭ 212866-70; 180 rooms; rates: average and above; reservations in Bangkok ℭ 2532641-2; telex: TH 65522 MERLIN). Considerably cheaper rooms are available at the **Thavorn Hotel**, (ℭ 211-333-5; 200 rooms; rates: moderate).

Laundry can be very expensive in the larger hotels. A good, cheap and fast service is provided in town by the **Bay Laundry** on Phuket Road.

AWAY FROM THE BEACHES

Phuket has some inland attractions as well. Seven kilometers (four miles) south of the town is the **Marine Biological Research Center** where some of the underwater beauties of the Andaman Sea can be examined at close quarters. Then north of the town, on the road to the airport, stands **Wat Phra Thong** with its half-buried golden Buddha. On your way there you will pass the **Heroines' Monument** commemorating the two women who led Phuket to victory against the encroaching Burmese in 1785.

To get to the **Ton Yai Waterfall**, turn right off the main road at Thalang, down a side road running between rubber plantations. Three kilometers on there is a large clearing in the forest, with a small lake where a river reaches the plain from the hills. Here a Nature Center and some refreshment stalls have been constructed. There are also some forlorn creatures — a Brahminy kite and some pig-tailed macaques — in cages. There's no admission fee.

The falls themselves are only small fingers of water trickling prettily over the rocks in the dry season. You can walk up half a kilometer or so into the jungle, but there are no falls to compare with what you'd find in even the most modest mountains. Nevertheless, it's a quiet and pleasant enough spot, suitable perhaps for a picnic if you're desperate for a change from the beach.

DIVING

Phuket is Thailand's major diving center. It offers varied inshore exploration round

marine creatures (such as reef sharks, rays and barracuda) due to the proximity of the edge of the continental shelf.

Phuket's diving centers for the most part congregate round Patong and Kata beaches. **Santana** has two premises, one between Kata and Karon beaches (℃ (076) 381598), the other at Patong (℃ (076) 321-360). Also between Kata and Karon are the **Siam Diving Centre** — with another office on Phi Phi Don — and **Marina Divers** (℃ (076) 381625; fax: 213604, Attn Marina).

the many nearby islands, notably **Koh Racha** (pronounced *raya* in Thai), **Shark Point**, and **Koh Doc Mai**, plus longer trips out to the Phi Phi Islands. Further away still, **Surin Island**, on the border of Thailand and Burma, also provides exceptionally fine diving opportunities.

But it is the celebrated **Similan Islands** that are for divers the finest jewels in the Andaman Sea's crown. They are 110 km (68 miles) north of Phuket and are a Marine National Park. They are uninhabited except for the Park Headquarters on one of the islands. Here the diving is world-class, with clear water up to 40 meters, excellent underwater growth, and large

At Patong there are the **South East Asia Yacht Charter Co.** (℃ (076) 321292; telex: 65542 SIMILAN TH) and the **Holiday Diving Club** (℃ (076) 212901-4, ext 029; fax: 321330, Attn Holiday Diving Club). All companies offer one-day initial instruction plus trial dives for beginners.

For non-diving trips out to the Similans, contact **Songserm Travel** (℃ (076) 214-297; fax: 214301).

Shopping center, Phuket Town. The town is a prosperous provincial center offering a change from the international tourist facilities of the beach resorts.

PHUKET'S CHINESE VEGETARIAN FESTIVAL

A Personal Memory

(Dates for the Vegetarian Festival vary from year to year as it's fixed according to the lunar calendar. But it's always at the end of September or in early October — TAT will inform you in advance of the dates for any particular year).

The man with the javelin protruding

equidistantly from each cheek stops, turns towards me, and waits for me to press the shutter. I do so, though by this time almost resignedly. He gives me a little bow, which causes the flesh to sag away from his eyes, and then rejoins the procession with what looks like a skip of pleasure.

It is Phuket's annual Chinese Vegetarian Festival, the nine days' autumn orgy of skewered cheeks, pierced tongues, ladders of knives and walking on fire.

As evening approaches I join a crowd making its way to one of the temples. The sky burns with a sultry tropical sunset as the sun sinks unhurriedly behind purple and crimson clouds.

During this period, many Thais join with the large local Chinese population in abstaining from meat, dressing in white, and paying daily visits to the various Chinese temples in Phuket town where the main ceremonies are staged.

In the temple forecourt boys are raking the coals in preparation to a broad rectangular bank and coaxing them into a dull glow with electric fans. Drums are being beaten, and there rises from the dense crowd an expectant hubbub.

As I walk up the steps an old man comes up to me and points his finger at my black T-shirt. "Black not so good," he says. Then "Black very bad!" Dismayed, I go down into the street and quickly buy a fancifully decorated white shirt for a few dollars. I put it on, and as I walk up the temple steps I am greeted on all sides by the incomparable smiles of Thai approval.

The men who are going to walk on the coals are striding about indiscriminately in the inner temple, naked except for elaborately wound loin-cloths. They are flexing their muscles, as if summoning up strength for the ordeal.

"Soon they will become into the monk," says my Thai friend. He keeps on saying it and I can't work out what he means.

Then the drums, gongs and bells increase in intensity to announce the beginning of the ceremony. I notice that the men are going in turn to a place at the back of the temple from which they return shaking their heads and with their eyes raised to the roof. Suddenly I realize what my friend had been trying to say. "They will become into the monk" means "The spirit will enter into them", in other words they will become "possessed". And as I watch the men crowd down the steps towards the fire, shaking and juddering as they go, I know that this is "possession by spirits" as travelers and anthropologists have described it in many parts of the world.

Then they begin. As the crowd presses forward and the photographers adjust their lenses, the thirty or so men begin to cross the now grey but gently smoking coals.

The older men stride across with a resolution bred of past experience, but the teenagers run across, and then stop to dance wildly for a moment, kicking the normally hostile element in disdain before jumping off and running round to join the queue for another crossing.

It is soon over. The drumming stops, the lights go on in the open-air theatre set up in a corner of the forecourt, and the pedlars and hawkers begin to jig their toy monkeys and plastic windmills for renewed business.

Travel round the bay is in low-lying long-tailed boats powered by out-board motors. Each seats about fourteen people, two abreast. Pineapples and eggs for delivery off-shore are piled aft. They leave the muddy creeks that wind their way through mangrove swamps, and enter the bay itself at considerable speed, throwing up coils of spray on either side.

The spectacular islands rise sheer to several hundreds of meters, like high-rise buildings in the sea. On the tops, tufts of

SOUTH FROM PHUKET

PHANG-NGA

This is a most spectacular bay 75 km (47 miles) from Phuket town. To get there you cross back onto the mainland and turn right. It's almost invariably visited as part of a conducted day-trip.

What is special about Phang-Nga is what is also special about the coast south of Phuket — towering limestone formations rising dramatically straight out of the sea. At Phang-Nga there's an impressive group of them contained in a largely untouched bay.

trees flourish incongruously. Sometimes the summits are in cloud.

Most trips pass under the craggy arch known as **Tam Lod Cave** where huge stalactites hang from the roof halfway to sea-level.

A stop is usually made at **Khoa Ping Gun**, "James Bond Island" to the Thais because one of the scenes of *The Man with the Golden Gun* was filmed here. Nowadays disconsolate locals wait to sell you shell jewelry, and there's really not a great deal to see.

Phuket Town — OPPOSITE: Portuguese-style houses show the influence of traders of old; ABOVE: a quick cool-off in the street is for some people the only real option. Note the local bus in the background.

Far more interesting is the Muslim village of **Pan Yee**. This is the regular lunch stop. The villagers do look rather jaded at having had their lives so changed by this daily tourist invasion — even so, it's a curious and marvelous place. The entire village is built on stilts stuck into the sea bed. The only settlement in this part of the wild and spectacular bay, the village is an extraordinary and impressive sight. But if you want a beer with your lunch you'll have to bring your own.

Superior accomodation is available at the **Phang Nga Bay Resort Hotel**, ℂ (076) 411067-70, rates: average and above; telex 67303 BAYHTL TH, reservations in Bangkok ℂ 3982543-4.

A Buddha Cave

Between Phuket and Phang-Nga are the caves at **Suwan Ku Ha**, and many of the day tours stop there. They're well worth seeing.

The first impression you get on entering the caves is of the squeaking of innumerable bats. From the opening at the foot of a cliff, the caves rise in a series, and a current of air ventilates them from lower to upper (the top cave is open to the sky).

Consequently it isn't until you are past the first cave, full of Buddhas and incense-sellers, that you encounter the foul smell of the bat-droppings. It's therefore as well to buy incense sticks and light them when the need arises.

Incised steps in the rock lead up to the last and narrowest cave, glistening white and lit by a shaft of sunlight.

This final, bat-less cave is a real treasure. Its shining rock formations are like swirling organ pipes, or, where they are flat and smoothed by aeons of water action, like perfectly arranged drapery. It's a natural temple, and, perhaps in recognition of this, the Thais have made no attempt to add any further, pious decoration.

Tourism has arrived very recently at Phi Phi Don, usually known simply as Phi Phi Island but in fact one of a pair of islands. The other, Phi Phi Lay, is uninhabited but very magnificent.

KRABI PROVINCE

Phi Phi Island

Phi Phi is a very attractive island group one and a quarter hours, 45 km, (28 miles) south of Phuket by the express boats. It's visually striking because it is largely made up of the kind of limestone seen most dramatically at Phang-Nga.

A Bird's Eye View

What is usually referred to as Phi Phi Island is actually Phi Phi Don. This is the island where everyone stays. Its sister island, Phi Phi Lay, is uninhabited, but incomparably more interesting.

Phi Phi Don village stands on a sandy strip between high limestone hills. It has two beaches, back to back to each other: it's only a three minute walk from the one to the other. Imagine a capital letter "H" and that's Phi Phi Don. The horizontal bar in the middle is the village, the two uprights the limestone hills, and the space between them the island's two beautiful bays.

Almost all the boats berth at the southeast side where there's a jetty and a small fishing fleet, but some of the boats bound for Krabi anchor out in the other, shallow bay and you may have to wade out with your bags under your arms even to get to the open boats that are going to take you out to the ferry itself.

If you arrive from Phuket you will certainly land at the jetty, and this is the place to take a general look at the island. Facing out to sea, the village proper, with its stores and fishermen's huts, is behind you. On your right are some of the better restaurants and bungalow hotels backed by high cliffs, while the coast stretches away to **Long Beach** to your left.

Where to Stay

There are several places where you can stay. The **PP Island Cabana** (rates: moderate), for example, is on the right in the first bay and has a good restaurant. Or, if you find you prefer the peaceful northwest

facing side, the **Krabi Pee Pee Resort** (rates: moderate) offers clean and quite comfortable rooms at half the price. The newest, and most luxurious hotel, is the **P.P. International Resort** (120 rooms; rates: expensive; reservations in Bangkok (255 8790-8).

Long Beach is where all the budget accommodation is, the **PP Paradise Pearl** (rates: inexpensive), for instance. These places are very basic, though, with no electricity and — at the time of writing — no

mosquito nets. But the snorkeling is close in-shore here, and there are new bungalows going up all the time. Boats will take you there from the harbor for 10 baht.

A Peaceful Place

Tourism has only very recently reached Phi Phi Don, and many people speak no English. But it's a place that shows you the life of a traditional fishing village in South East Asia at closer quarters than you'll find in the more developed resorts. Though the areas you can stay in are restricted by nature, the island nevertheless provides a restful ambiance.

But the real attraction of this pair of islands is Phi Phi Lay.

Homage To Phi Phi Lay

The uninhabited island of Phi Phi Lay stands next to Phi Phi Don and is one of the world's major sources of birds' nests of the kind used to make the celebrated Chinese delicacy, bird's nest soup. One

company has the concession to harvest the immensely lucrative nests, and no commercial development is allowed on the island that might disturb the birds and cause them to nest elsewhere. Nevertheless, the snorkeling nearby is unparalleled, and day or half-day trips can be arranged, with landing permitted on the one beach on the island's north side. The so-called "Viking" drawings on the cave walls are of unknown origin, but Viking they are certainly not.

From the sea, Phi Phi Lay presents a striking outline. Its sombre peaks rise up sheer from the water, and as you approach you feel in harmony with the poets who have written that the sea is death, vast, formless and engulfing.

Soon you see the ropes and long bamboos used to get at the precious nests. The boatman pulls the long boat with difficulty up against the cliff, next to a rough landing stage projecting from the cave's mouth. You clamber up and walk along planks into the cave. It's like entering a pirate's lair.

The cave is like a cathedral, and the high bamboo structures appear like religious totems, or items from a bizarre constructionist theater-set. These structures reach into the upper dark and are really just bundles of very long bamboos tied together with string, the string providing the footholds for the climbers. The only light is what comes from the cave mouth.

The overall impression is that of Piranesi's *Carcieri* engravings, of a place both forbidding and awesome, and symbolic of a great and impenetrable mystery.

In corners stand petrified limestone cascades, resembling side-altars where a myriad candles have been burned for centuries, their wax falling to make elaborate formal structures.

At first you don't see the birds. But you hear them, and smell their droppings. They nest high up, like bats, in the dark vault of the cave. The invisible nature of the secret work in the cave makes it seem eerie as well as impressive. Lone plum-colored insects crawl on the guano. From outside comes the sound of the sea endlessly washing against the cave's mouth.

Number One

After the cave, a tour round the island will take you into an enclosed bay, almost a womb. "Number one!" announces the boatman.

And indeed it is Number One. You enter between high cliffs, as if into the jaws of death. The water is an unreal green. Limestone turrets and pinnacles topped with dwarf shrubs form the skyline. It's a site for a performance of a Wagner Ring Cycle opera, or for a private audience with The Immortals.

Great stacks of land follow. Now the rock's color begins to come on display — orange smudges on ochre cliffs. Then, as you come into the shadow of the north side of the island, more strips of bamboo structure begin to appear high above you aimed at darkly stained, remote cave mouths, caves like bubbles in a block of ice that has been shattered open with a knife.

The sides of the island are everywhere wholly inhospitable and sheer, with the exception of the very occasional minute beach at the foot of the cliffs. But, inside another, less forbidding enclave, there is the island's one beach of any size, sandy, and with a couple of thatched huts backed up against the cliff. This is where snorkelers make their base, and by midday it's usually crowded with day-trippers, an unwelcome violation of the island's solemnity.

Moving on, the formations of the limestone itself are staggering. Stalactites hang from every protuberance, stained black underneath as in a sooty Victorian railway station. Here and there trees, locked into rocky clefts, flourish with a strange delicacy of leaf and branch. In one place a column has crashed into the sea, and its spiny roots of rock stand exposed and ruddy in the dark shadows.

Then you pull away into the open sea, the boatman hauling on the long motor handle to keep the craft on course. And you cross over back to Phi Phi Don. But the coastline is at first very like Phi Phi Lay's and more nests became visible, almost glutinous now, like threads of solidified toffee hanging off a spoon.

Here on Phi Phi Don there is yet another enclosed amphitheater, smaller than those on Phi Phi Lay and less formidable. At the head of this bay there is another cave. This one goes in long and deep. Oil lamps generally stand in the entrance, but you need to bring your own matches.

Boat Hire

Boats can be hired on Phi Phi Don — the standard rate often quoted is 600 baht a day, 400 baht a half day, per boat-load. But deals can sometimes be struck for less.

Boats leave Phi Phi Don for Krabi several times a day. You can either take the "express" boat (one and a half hours) for 125 baht, or the regular one (two hours) for 100 baht.

Bookings for this, as for other excursions, can be made with the very reliable **Friendship Tours** at the harbor.

PHI PHI TO KRABI

This trip passes further magnificent limestone stacks — forested turrets and wholly inaccessible fortresses of sheer stone.

OPPOSITE: the so-called 'Viking Cave' on Phi-Phi Lay, a major source of birds' nests for the soup so loved and valued throughout the Chinese world. The cave is a twenty-minute boat trip from Phi-Phi Don, the main island. ABOVE: Fishing boats in the Gulf of Siam.

They're forms the imagination can easily populate — the lairs of beasts elsewhere long extinct, or the haunts where terrorized souls at last find their beleaguered rest. As you enter the Krabi estuary, they become if anything even more wonderful, jutting tigerishly out over the sea, walls of rock stained only with their own natural coloration, isolated stumps like beached mines — but 200 m (660 ft) high.

And these stalactited culinary bird's nest sites — found here too — look as if some haggard witch has retreated into an elevated cave and hung out her tattered lace curtains to dry — only in reality it's all of stone.

The fast boat goes to Krabi, but the regular one puts its passengers ashore at Ao Nang, a beach half an hour's dusty bus journey from the town.

Ao Nang

This is a fine beach with spectacular marine views, a much nicer place to stay than Krabi itself. There's accommodation on the seafront at **Ao Nang Villa** (rates: inexpensive), or a little way inland at **Princess Garden** (14 rooms; rates: inexpensive). The **Krabi Resort** (℃ (075) 611389; 80 rooms; rates: average and above; reservations in Bangkok ℃ 2518094) offers luxury accommodation.

A Shell Cemetery

Between Ao Nang and Krabi is the unspectacular **Shell Cemetery**. At the foot of a small headland, paving-stone-like slabs of rock lie broken on the shore. It's called a "cemetery" only because the slabs of rock could be imagined as fallen gravestones.

These pieces of horizontal strata are actually made of compacted sea shells estimated to be 75 million years old. Despite the probable age of huge amounts of the earth's surface, this particular feat of dating has, it seems, caught the imaginatio⸱ of the tour organizers, and the flat top oᴸ the headland is a mass of food-stalls and souvenir shops (selling, incidentally, some very beautiful shells).

The "cemetery" is rather difficult to get to by public transport, though plenty of tours go there. It's 17 km (11 miles) from Krabi, but six or so from the main road where the buses run. Boatmen will bring you from Ao Nang (100 baht maximum), or you can arrange to be brought by motorbike from Krabi, or charter a minibus.

The whole coastline north of Krabi is a magnificent assembly of untouched sandy beaches, backed by forest and the ubiquitous partially-wooded limestone stacks. Many of these beaches are only easily accessible by boat and while this remains the case it's unlikely that commercial tourism will establish a foothold. But you can't be sure — its tentacles are ever-expanding.

KRABI TOWN

Krabi Province may be grand and untouched, but the town itself has little to recommend it.

To look at, Krabi Town is just four blocks of concrete, two-story offices and shops, with a cinema, a Post Office, one good travel agent and a tolerable hotel. The town fronts onto the river estuary where there's a pier from which boats leave for Phi Phi Island.

There's also a night-market of sorts (largely daytime shops that stay open late), and a couple of massage parlours recognizable by the exceptionally dimly-lit coffee-shops which form their lobbies and the fairy-lights that festoon their doors.

Comfortable accommodation is available at the **Phra Nang Inn** (℃ (075) 612173-4; fax: 612251; 62 rooms; rates: moderate), and there is also the plain but satisfactory **Thai Hotel** (℃ (07) 611474-5; 100 rooms; rates: moderate) with its inappropriately flash coffee-shop. There are also several very unprepossessing but inexpensive guest houses.

The exceptionally helpful **Pee Pee Tours and Transport Corporation Limited** (at

A fishing village on the southern Thai coast. Note the light-weight, airy character of the buildings, the widespread use of corrugated iron for roofs, the habit of building on stilts for coolness and as a protection against damp and insects, and the endemic poverty. Note too, in the foreground, the garbage.

31 Prachachoen Road; ℂ (075) 612155) will book travel to Trang, Had Yai, Bangkok, Malaysia or Singapore, as well as to Phi Phi Island, and will cheerfully give you free advice on other services from which they don't stand to make any profit — always a good sign.

Krabi is the capital of Krabi Province. For more information on the three south-western provinces of Krabi, Trang and Satun, see the OFF THE BEATEN TRACK Section.

KRABI TO HAT YAI

By bus, this journey takes four and a half hours and the fare is 60 baht. The buses come from Phuket and don't go into Krabi itself — you have to go five kilometers (three miles) out of Krabi Town to the main road (minibuses leave from near the Thai Hotel for the main road every 15 minutes — 4 baht).The last bus of the day along the main road for Hat Yai goes at 2 pm.

If you decide to stop overnight at Trang (see OFF THE BEATEN TRACK), you can get a non air-conditioned bus from Trang to Hat Yai next day from outside the Thumrin Hotel on the hour — fare 30 baht.

HAT YAI

Twenty years ago an insignificant frontier market, Hat Yai is today a remarkably vigorous and even sophisticated place. The reason for this is the prosperity of neighboring Malaysia and Singapore. Thailand is the prime holiday destination for these countries, and Hat Yai is quite simply the first town they come to. If what they are looking for is primarily sex and secondarily cheap shopping, they have no need to venture any further.

If they do find time for other pleasures, then there is the coastal resort of Songkhla, 30 km (19 miles) down the road. Songkhla by day and Hat Yai at night is a common weekend visitors' formula in these parts.

GETTING THERE

Hat Yai is 947 km (593 miles) south of Bangkok. Flying time is one and a quarter hours and there are two flights a day, with additional flights at weekends. The airport is 11 km (seven miles) from the town. When in Hat Yai, contact Thai Airways for details on ℂ 245851-2.

By rail, Hat Yai is 16 hours from the capital. Comfortable overnight trains leave in the late afternoon in each direction. The line also continues south into Malaysia, through Butterworth (for Penang), Kuala Lumpur, and ends up in Singapore. Hat Yai railway station is on Ratakarn Road, ℂ 244362.

Buses run just about everywhere, including south to Singapore and Malaysia. For details phone Hat Yai ℂ 232789, or any travel agent.

WHERE TO STAY

Accommodation in Hat Yai begins with the fine **JB Hotel** (ℂ (074) 234300-18, fax: (074) 243499; 209 rooms; rates: expensive; reservations in Bangkok ℂ 258 2663). Situated a two minute drive from the town center, it's the best hotel in town with a wide range of facilities including a swimming pool and tennis court.

Among the many others are the **Grand Plaza** (ℂ (074) 243760; 145 rooms; rates: moderate; telex: 62118 GP), comfortable and particularly good value; **The Regency** (ℂ (074) 234400-9; 189 rooms; rates: moderate); the **Montien** (ℂ (074) 246968-9; 180 rooms; rates: moderate); the **Sukhontha** (ℂ (074) 243999; 205 rooms; rates: moderate), and the rather more basic **Hat Yai International** (ℂ (074) 231022; 210 rooms; rates: moderate).

A remote cove on Phi Phi Don.

RESTAURANTS

There are many places to eat in Hat Yai — recommended are the **Sukhontha Bakery and Coffee Shop** (real coffee) on Saneh Anusorn Road, and the **Krua Luang** round the corner on Pracha Thipat Road. There are excellent restaurants in major hotels such as the JB.

For cheap late-night eating, Hat Yai has four **night markets**. They're situated as

gigantic Buddha image. This last is here reclining, and is claimed to be the third largest in this position in the world. It's 35 m (115 ft) long and 15 m (49 ft) high, and at the time of writing is being given a glittering new roof.

But what you shouldn't miss is the aerial cableway that, with whirring claxon, and originally, and perhaps soon once again, flashing lights, conveys tiles paid for by devotees' donations up to the roof. The celestial chariot is drawn by two plastic

follows: (1) close to the President Hotel and the nearby Bus Station (the biggest); (2) near Wat Chu Chan on Supphasan Rangsan Road; (3) at Chee Uthit Road; (4) at the intersection of Sri Poowanat Road and Tan Ratanakorn Road.

WAT HAT YAI NAI

There are few tourist sights of the traditional kind in Hat Yai. Wat Hat Yai Nai is distinguished by its gimmicks. It's a short distance from the town center, on Petch Kasem Road, and for the most part follows the usual Thai arrangement of food stalls, monks' living quarters and a

horses. It only takes a small donation for the attendant to be persuaded to give it a whirl.

You can alternatively place your offering in one — or all — of the bowls of ten life-size model monks, clasping their begging bowls and rotating in a circle propelled by electric motor. They alone make a visit essential.

GOLF

Four kilometers (three miles) out of town there's the 18-hole **Kho Hong Army Camp Golf Course**. Green fees are: Monday — Friday 100 baht; Saturday, Sunday and

Public Holidays 150 baht. Phone ☏ (074) 243605 for more information. It seems you cannot hire clubs there.

ATTRACTIONS

Shopping and Nightlife

The shopping is centered on the three parallel roads, Niphat Uthit 1, Niphat Uthit 2 and Niphat Uthit 3, and there's a night bazaar on Saneh Anusorn Road. Clothes and imported electronic goods are the attractions.

There's an immense variety of nightlife in Hat Yai, from hotel lounges and coffee shops with live music, to discos and massage parlors. The JB Hotel (see above for hotel details) has its **Palm Court** restaurant with constant music, Thai and Western, as well as its own **Metropolis Disco Club**. The Montien Hotel has its **Cetus Night Club**, and the International Hotel its popular **Inter Disco Club**. The Sukhontha Hotel's large **Zodiac Disco** offers a gay night on Thursdays.

The best known massage parlor is probably the **Pink Lady Massage and Coffee Shop** (behind the Sukhontha Hotel; ☏ 244095), and beauty centers, Turkish baths, "ancient massage" and health centers are not difficult to find.

Bull Fights

Southern Thai bull-fighting, a test of strength between two bulls and not a Spanish-style ritual slaughter, can be seen at one of two arenas — near the Nora Hotel on Tamnon Vithi Road on the first Sunday of the month, and out near the Hat Yai airport on the second Sunday.

GETTING ABOUT

Transport within Hat Yai is by open-back pick-ups. In effect they're shared taxis on the Malaysian pattern. Get in one that already has other passengers in it and you'll get where you want to go, but not necessarily by the shortest route, for 4 baht; get in an empty one and you'll be deemed to have "chartered" it — you'll get directly to your destination, and the fare will be 10 baht.

The system for taking a taxi out of town is as follows. Go to the President Hotel, a couple of minutes' walk north of the Bus Terminus. Opposite the hotel entrance is a car park, and a wooden cafe where the drivers wait. Tell a driver where you want to go — preferably have it written down in Thai beforehand — and you'll be shown to a car which you'll eventually share with other passengers.

Fares are very reasonable — the 60 km (37 miles), for instance, to the Waterbird Sanctuary at Thale Luang (Khu Khut) is 30 baht (see page 146). You pay before you leave. Drivers will try to extract a higher fare from foreigners, but if you show you know the approximate rate (ask at your hotel, or TAT) they'll be keen to take it from you. Transport is by saloon cars as opposed to open-backed city taxis. It's not a bad idea to take a quick look at the tyres before you set off.

Ton Nga Chang

A popular excursion from Hat Yai is to **Ton Nga Chang Waterfall**, 26 km (16 miles) south-west of the town. A direct minibus leaves from close to the Plaza Shopping Mall.

A river descends via seven cascades through a large upland area that is also a wildlife sanctuary. It's a short walk from the parking area to the first three falls, and it's at the third, where the river divides into two streams, fancifully compared to an elephant's tusks, that most people stop. Above here the track becomes more difficult. The time to see the

east. Furthermore, although the town appears to come to an end at the rocky point marked by a statue of a mermaid opposite the Samila Hotel, this is not in fact the tip of the spur, as might be expected; instead, it extends again to end in a sandy spit some way further to the north. For views of Songkhla's intriguing location, climb the rough path past the monkeys up **Khao Noi**, not far from the hotel.

Yet despite its interesting situation, there's little to see in the town. The

falls at their best is, naturally, in the rainy season.

TOURIST INFORMATION

There's a helpful **TAT** office at 1/1 Soi 2 Niphat Uthit 3, ((243747).

SONGKHLA

Before going to **Songkhla,** it's a good idea to take a look at the map. The town is situated on a spur, but rather than jutting out to sea, this serves to divide a large lake to the west from the open sea on the

Samila Hotel, ((311310-4, fax: 311314; 70 rooms; rates: average and above), gazes out to sea, and some undistinguished seafood restaurants cluster round it. Behind the hotel there's a miniature topiary garden, part of a bigger park, that isn't worth a first glance, let alone a second. And in front of the hotel there's the bronze mermaid fixed to the rocks so it can be photographed with off-shore islands **Maew** and **Nu** ("cat" and "mouse") in the background.

OPPOSITE and ABOVE: highly-decorated fishing boats such as these can be seen in many places in the Muslim south, from Songkhla's Kao Seng village down into Yala Province.

SAMILA BEACH

Extending to the left of the hotel and backed by pines, this is extensive and sandy, and some over-worked ponies provide fuel for the professional beach-photographers' ever-ready cameras. (There is another beach, equally sandy, on the hotel's left). Samila itself merges into the long spit of **Son On Cape**, with its deck chairs and sea-food restaurants.

KAO SENG

If you get on a *songthaew* down the long beach running south from (to the right of) the hotel, you will eventually come to a small Muslim fishing village, **Kao Seng**, on the left. Here elaborately painted fishing boats are worth seeing, and though most are well-weathered there are usually one or two newly refurbished ones that will tempt anyone's camera.

THE HARBOR

The large-scale modern fishing, though, gets done at the **harbor** on the other side of town. To see the barrels of fish and the colorful scene that surrounds them, take a "taxi" (3 baht) to Wichianchom Road and

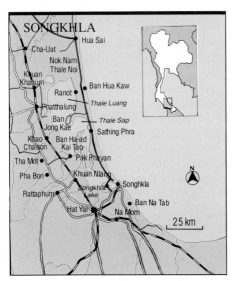

walk down one of the *sois*, for instance Soi 5. Near here, too, is the ferry over to **Koh Yoh** where hand-woven cotton goods are produced and can, of course, be bought.

SONGKHLA NATIONAL MUSEUM

This is situated on the campus of the Srinakharinvirot University, four kilometers (three miles) out of town. There are 11 rooms displaying objects from the region's rich past. One wing houses a collection of ceramics from archaeological sites from all over Thailand. The building itself is interesting as an example of nineteenth century southern Thai Chinese architecture. Opening hours are 9 am to noon, and 1 pm to 4 pm, Wednesday to Sunday (closed Monday and Tuesday.)

THALE LUANG WATERBIRD SANCTUARY

The water Songkhla's main harbor fronts onto is the seaward end of **Thale Luang**, Thailand's biggest lake. It extends womb-like up into the land, and is the breeding ground for a huge bird population. A vast area — 364 sq km (142 square miles) — has been declared a Waterbirds Sanctuary, Asia's largest. It contains 219 recorded bird species, including purple herons, purple gellinules, teals, grebes, egrets, cormorants and black-winged stilts. The Headquarters is a 60 km (37 miles) drive from Hat Yai, but it's well worth the effort of getting there.

The sky reflects in the shallow water, birds bat across towards the reedbeds, white egrets rise, dragonflies hover and moorhens hurry away in the langorous heat. In the distance are the high cow-horn gables of temples. From Headquarters you purr off in a long-tailed boat across the brilliant reflective surface of the lake.

The water is only inches deep. Isolated trees stand like sculptures above the surface. Colors are pale green, pale blue and

Fishing nets in the south — suspended from bamboos, they're raised and lowered at will.

The South and Phuket

the yellow of the reeds. With colors so delicate and reminiscent of northern pellucidities, it's very un-Thai.

The heat is intense. Pairs of ducks skidland, and boys in straw hats pole punts, shadowy behind reeds. The guides meander their way along the channels, and occasionally accelerate and surge across a reedy barrier with a cheer. Dawn and sunset, of course, are the times to see any birds; even so, there's plenty to see in the middle of thé day as well.

Back at Headquarters, the boys pole the punt silently under the stilted house. Inland, a cock crows, a radio launches into a sweet Thai pop tune, you walk on wooden slats to a simple restaurant, and the impression everywhere is of a perfect tranquillity and contentment.

More birds can be seen at the head of Songkhla Great Lake, at **Thale Noi Nok Nam** near Phatthalung (on the railway, north from Hat Yai).

YALA PROVINCE

Hat Yai is close to the Malaysian frontier on the western coast, but here in the east Thailand extends south another 200 km (134 miles) south in **Yala Province**, famous for the **town mosque** at **Pattani**, the painted fishing boats of **Panare Beach**, and, last of all, the border town of **Sungei Golok**, sensuously welcoming whether you're coming from the north, or, like most of its patrons, from the south.

Muslim schoolgirls in the far southeast.

Chiang Mai and the North

HILL TERRITORY

The north of Thailand has an immense amount to recommend it.

To begin with, the climate is less humid than anywhere else in the country, and, after prolonged exposure to the clammy south, to step out of the night-train from Bangkok into the cool morning air of Chiang Mai is a joy with few equals.

Chiang Mai, too, is an very attractive place. Though it's Thailand's second city, it's far smaller than Bangkok, and with few of the capital's horrors, environmental and otherwise. The atmosphere is relaxed, prices are reasonable, and the people particularly friendly and informal.

The north, too, contains some wonderful countryside. It's hill territory, and thinly populated except in the major valleys. The Thais themselves have for the most part kept to the fertile lowlands, and the hills are inhabited by the famous non-Thai hill-tribes.

The area is not without its problems. Opium poppies are still being grown here and this, together with the fact that the Burmese government does not exercise full control over its territory adjacent to the frontier, and official relations between Thailand and Laos are frequently strained, means that the area as a whole is not quite as settled in its ways as the central Thai provinces.

Nevertheless, tourism flourishes, and though there have been incidents of attacks on river boats carrying foreigners, the Thai government, with the high priority it puts on maintaining international tourism to the country, is determined to do all it can to prevent recurrences. It's a wonderful part of the country, and not to be missed, but it's wise to take care, and try not to be too conspicuous, particularly conspicuously affluent, in the remoter places.

The life of the countryside penetrates everywhere in the north. OPPOSITE: newly-planted rice fields reflect the sky; ABOVE: home from work.

PHITSANULOK

Not many people visit **Phitsanulok**, 390 km (244 miles) north of Bangkok. But it's half way between Bangkok and Chiang Mai, it's on the railway, and so makes a reasonable stopping-off point if you feel you don't want to rush the journey north. It's an important provincial capital, and has an airport with a daily flight from Bangkok. But the real attraction is

neighboring Sukhothai, 58 km (36 miles) away.

Thais know Phitsanulok for the Buddha image in **Wat Phra Si Rattana Mahathat**. Cast in 1357 in the reign of King Mahatammaracha of Sukhothai, it's considered the most beautiful Buddha-image in Thailand and copies of it can be seen just about everywhere.

Otherwise, the town has nothing remarkable besides the custom of cooks flinging food from the cooking pan up into the air, to be caught by a waiter standing with a plate some distance away. This bizarre habit can be observed outside several of the town's restaurants.

All rooms at the **Amarin Nakhon Hotel** (((055) 258588; 124 rooms; rates: moderate) are air-conditioned.

There's a **TAT** office in Phitsanulok — ((055) 252742.

SUKHOTHAI

Sukhothai was Thailand's first capital. The Thais are thought to have come south from China (see THE SIAMESE WORLD section) and so it isn't surprising their capital was first in the north, and only later moved south to Ayutthaya, and later Bangkok.

Modern Sukhothai is a pleasant country town — the extensive remains of the old capital are situated 12 km (8 miles) to the north. Neither is on the railway and the usual way to get there is by bus from Phitsanulok. If you want to stay overnight in the area, the **Rat Thani** (((055) 611031; rates: moderate) in the modern town has air-conditioned rooms.

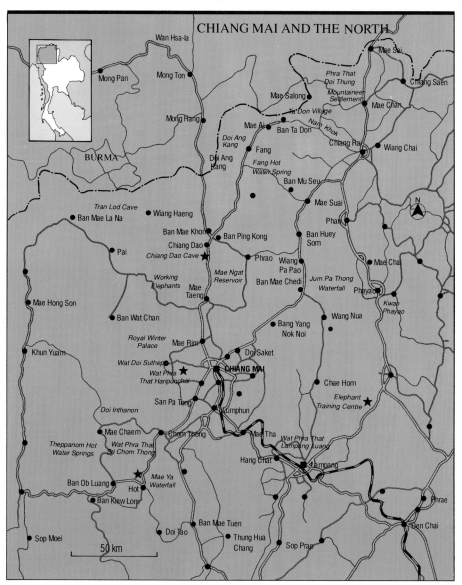

CHIANG MAI AND THE NORTH

Old Sukhothai is like Ayutthaya — ruined and semi-ruined monuments standing forlornly, but still with traces of magnificence, in dry grassland criss-crossed nowadays only with footpaths. There is a central Headquarters, housing administrative offices both of the Thai government Fine Arts Department and of UNESCO who are helping in the work of reconstruction and preservation. Sukhothai is considered a site of world significance.

The remains extend over a wide area, but there are fine things to see close to the Headquarters building if you decide to allocate only a small amount of your time to the site.

THE SUKHOTHAI ERA

The period during which Sukhothai was the Thai capital was 1238 to 1365. Originally the Thais formed small principalities in what is now northern Thailand, but in the early thirteenth century two of these combined to fight the powerful Khmer Empire to their south. They won, and established a combined capital in the former Khmer frontier post of Sukhothai. The event is now taken as marking the establishment of the first Thai kingdom, and essentially the foundation of the state of Thailand.

The third Sukhothai ruler, King Ramkamheng, extended the power of the new kingdom even beyond the country's modern borders in this northern region. He established trade relations with China and visited the country twice, the first time to negotiate with the great Kubla Kahn. Chinese artists came back to Sukhothai with him and established the **Sawankalok School** of Thai pottery.

King Ramkamheng also oversaw the creation of the modern Thai alphabet from various old Khmer scripts. A famous inscription of the period carved in stone reads: "This City of Sukhothai is good. There are fish in the water, there is rice in the fields. The king does not tax people who ride the road to market, leading their oxen and their horses. Whoever wants to trade in elephants does so, whoever wants to trade in silver

and gold does so." The fact that it was discovered inside the Royal Palace, though, might indicate it was a piece of self-promotion by the illustrious monarch himself.

Sukhothai's time of glory passed when, after 127 years, it became subject to the new and more powerful kingdom of Ayutthaya in the south.

THE RUINS

The remains at Sukhothai are spread over

a wide area. Many of the main ones are concentrated within the square central "walled city", with others scattered at some distance in all four directions.

Inside the walled area, the **Royal Palace and Wat Mahathat** is surrounded by a moat. There isn't much left of the palace, but the huge *wat* contains many semi-ruined *chedis* in the lotus-bud shape characteristic of the Sukhothai style. Other temple remains in this central compound are **Wat Traphang-Thong**, **Wat Sa-Si**, and **Wat Traphang-Ngoen**.

One place that can help you orient yourself is the **Ramkamheng National Museum**. It's in the central area and is open 9 am to noon and 1 to 4 pm; closed Mondays, Tuesdays and official holidays.

Other sites are difficult to get to — it's best to get advice from the Headquarters before attempting a trip out to them.

Austere and august – the extensive and large-scale ruins of Wat Mahathat in ancient Sukhothai.

It may seem that ancient Sukhothai has little to offer in anything approaching its original state. This is true, and the reasons are that the city was sacked when it fell in 1365, that the tropical climate is not ideal for the preservation of anything, and that what valuable items remained have for the most part been removed and put in museums.

LAMPANG

Mention Lampang to the average Thai and he'll think of horse-drawn carriages. Mention it to most tourists and, if they think of anything at all, they'll probably think of baby elephants.

Horses still provide a regular means of transport round the small town, but you'll need something more powerful to get you to the **Young Elephant Training Center**. It's situated 54 km (34 miles) to the northeast, on the road to Phayao (though there are plans to move it to between Lampang and Lumphun).

The small elephants, only as big as a medium-sized dog at birth, are taught like children. Their "school" has summer holidays (from March to May), is closed on religious festivals, subjects its pupils to primary education between the years of three and five, and secondary between six and ten.

They then begin their working lives at 11, doing apprentice work until they are 16, by which time they are considered adult members of the community. Their official retirement age is 61.

Demonstrations — of assembly, communal bathing, log-rolling and carrying, and piling logs — are given every morning (though not on festival days, or during the two month summer vacation). Hotels and tour agents in Lampang will make all the arrangements necessary to get you up there.

There are several unassuming hotels in Lampang. The **Tip Chang** (℡ (054) 218078;

Dreaming of ages long past — a Buddha silhouetted against the evening sky at Sukhothai's Wat Mahathat.

125 rooms; rates: moderate) provides air-conditioned accommodation.

Lampang is on the main Bangkok–Chiang Mai railway, and can also be reached by bus from Chiang Mai.

CHIANG MAI

Thailand's second city, 761 km (472 miles) by train north of Bangkok, is a lot smaller than the capital and very much more

international airport, and its station is the northern terminus of the rail system.

The original walled and moated city was completed in 1296 as the capital of the then independent Lannathai kingdom. The Burmese seized it in due course, along with most of what is now northern Thailand, but it has been Thai territory continuously since 1774.

Over the centuries the city has shifted eastwards, and what is remarkable is how comparatively uninteresting the area en-

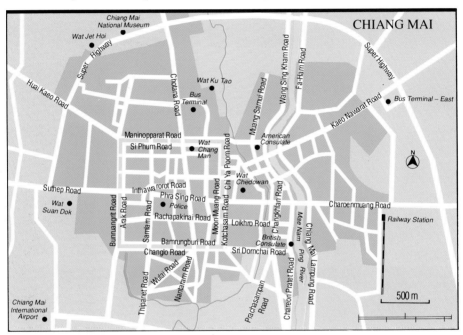

CHIANG MAI

congenial. There has been little high-rise development, temples and wooden houses stand alongside modern hotels in the central area, and pedicabs are still a viable means of transport.

A BIRD'S EYE VIEW

The city is sited on the broad plain of the Mae Ping River. Some 30 km (18 miles) wide, this plain is the major level area in what is otherwise rough hill country. Prominent in all views from the city is the dramatically-located temple of Doi Suthep, perched high in the hills overlooking the town. Chiang Mai has a domestic and

closed by the old walls now is. The heart of modern Chiang Mai is the area that lies between the east wall and the river. This is not just a recent development — several old temples are to be found here.

The walls of the old city have recently been re-built. Antiquarians may grumble, but throughout Thai history things that have been valued have been maintained, and few will complain when the result is as magnificent as it is in the vicinity of Tha Phae Gate (at the top end of Tha Phae Road).

Chiang Mai is celebrated for the friendliness and beauty of its people, for its rich cultural heritage, and as the center from which to organize treks out to the rivers and hills that surround it.

WHERE TO STAY

The premier Chiang Mai hotel, used by the government for putting up heads of state, is the **Chiang Mai Orchid** (℃ (053) 222099; fax: 221625; 265 rooms; rates: average and above). The **Rincome** (℃ (053) 221044; fax: 221915; 158 rooms; rates: average and above) is even nicer, tranquil and exquisitely decorated. The **Dusit Inn** (℃ (053) 251033-6; fax: 251037; 200 rooms; rates: average and above) and the **Chiang Inn** (℃ (053) 235655; fax: 234299; 170 rooms; rates: average and above) are also in the luxury class, as is the **Chiang Mai Plaza** (℃ (053) 270040; fax: 252230; 242 rooms; rates: average and above). Note that prices are everywhere noticeably lower here than in Bangkok.

The **Pornping** (℃ (053) 270100-7; 328 rooms; rates: average and above) is also very comfortable. The **River View Lodge** (℃ (053) 271110; fax: 249019; 36 rooms; rates: moderate) is a family hotel with a beautiful setting on the banks of the Mae Ping, while a good bet for the visitor wanting something simple but central, clean and air-conditioned, would be the **Montri** (℃ (053) 211069; fax: 217416; 80 rooms; rates: moderate).

In the budget-price category there is a wide choice. The area to look is essentially around Tha Phae Gate. The **New Chiang Mai Hotel** (℃ (053) 236561; 43 rooms; rates: inexpensive) on Chiyapoom Road is a basic Thai-style place with few foreigners in evidence. **Happy House** (℃ (053) 234969) also changes money at all hours. Others in this area are the **Top North,** ℃ (053) 213900, the **Sumit,** ℃ (053) 211033, and the **Satum,** ℃ (053) 211575, guest houses.

There are more budget-category hotels attractively sited on the river bank. Cross the river from the down-town area by the Nakornping Bridge and take the first road on your left. Among these are the **Je T'Aime,** ℃ (053) 241912, the **Hollanda-Montri,** ℃ (053) 242450, and the **Gold River Side,** ℃ (053) 244550.

Visitors should not expect too much from these very inexpensive places where the over-night charge can be as low as US$2.

RESTAURANTS

The Chalet, ℃ (053) 236310, on Chareon Pratet Road offers quality French cuisine in a Northern-style teak house.

The **Whole Earth** Thai food and vegetarian restaurant, ℃ (053) 232463, is on Sridonchai Road. It's in the middle-bracket as far as prices go and serves ten types of real coffee.

Just out of town, the **Baan Suan,** ℃ (053) 242116, has tables on lawns under the trees and tends to cater to the more up-market coach parties. Birds sing, sprinklers hiss and corks pop. Look for the knife and fork sign on the right, 500 m after the first silk factory on the road out to Borsarng.

Wat Phra Singh, Chiang Mai. Begun in the fourteenth century, the temple is famous for the ancient Buddha image kept there.

Traditional *khantok* dinners (eaten with the hands to the accompaniment of local dances) can be had at, among other places, the **Khumkaeo Palace** (℃ (053) 214315. **The Chalet** (℃ (053) 236310) offers traditional French cuisine in a Northern-style teak house, and the **Whole Earth** (℃ (053) 232463) has good quality vegetarian food. Just out of town, the **Baan Suan** (℃ (053) 242116) has tables on lawns under trees — birds sing, sprinklers hiss and corks pop. Also out of town is the **Chiangmai Lakeside Ville** (℃ (01) 5100258) where you can eat — and stay — in a Thai ambiance beside a small artificial lake. Japanese food is on offer at the **Musashi Restaurant** (℃ (053) 210944) and Arabic at **The Cafeteria** (℃ (053) 235276) near the Night Bazaar. There's live music — folk and blues — at the **Riverside** (℃ (053) 243239) opposite the Chinda Hospital, and a congenial atmosphere at **Bier Stube** (℃ (053) 210869) on Moon Muang Road, with reasonably priced cocktails, beer and substantial German and Thai food. **Daret's House** (℃ (053) 235440) is an excellent, cheap and deservedly popular outdoor eating place close to the Tha Phae Gate. (They also run a guest-house and motor-bike rental service). Nowadays, however, they are experiencing severe competition from the Montien Hotel's smarter, air-conditioned **JJ Bakery** opposite.

A CITY TOUR

The town itself can easily be explored on your own. It's quite small enough, and flat enough, to hire a bicycle and just pedal round. If this seems too much like hard work, there are motorbike hire establishments on every street corner, though the traffic can be just a touch too heavy for absolute beginners.

Chiang Mai's Wat Jet Yot. The temple is celebrated for its "Indian style", but all southeast Asian culture is deeply influenced by India, both its religions and its resulting artistic forms.

A day's sightseeing should take in at least some of the following. First **Wat Phra Singh**, with its fine grounds. Then **Wat Je Dee Luang**, with its large fifteenth-century *chedi* (Je Dee = chedi), and **Wat Chang Man** with its tiny Crystal Buddha, all in the walled district.

Then there's the seven-spired **Wat Jet Yot**, built to an Indian model to the northwest, close to the Super Highway. Nearby is the **Chiang Mai National Museum**, open daily from 9 am to noon, 1 to 4 pm, except Mondays and Tuesdays.

Finally, **Wat Suan Dok** off Suthep Road to the west has some striking wall-paintings, and the **Night Bazaar**, close to the Chiang Inn and Suriwongse hotels, serves to round off the day. Near the bazaar, the mural across the front of the Sang Tawan Cinema on Sri Dornchai Road (by the Whole Earth restaurant) is worth a few minutes' admiring gaze.

SHOPPING

Northern Thailand is famous for its crafts, and almost all the craft shopping in Chiang Mai — for silk, silver, lacquerware, wood-carvings and hill-tribe crafts — is out on the Borsang road. The village of Borsang itself is where painted umbrellas are made and sold. See under SHOPPING FOR CRAFTS (p. 163) and BORSANG — UMBRELLA VILLAGE (p. 165) for details.

The two biggest bookshops in Chiang Mai are the **Suriwong Book Center** on Sri Dornchai Road and **D.K.Books** on Tha Phae Road.

The **Library Service**, ℃ (053) 210518, on Ratchamankha Soi 2, off Moon Muang Road, has a selection of second-hand English, German and other books for sale. They can be sold back later at half-price.

NIGHT LIFE

Chiang Mai is rather well known among Thais for its night life as it's a popular destination for long weekends out of Bangkok.

Discos in the big hotels include **Club 77** in the Chiang Mai Orchid, **Bubbles** in the Pornping, and the **Plaza Disco** in the Chiang Mai Plaza.

Honey Massage, situated on the Superhighway, near the Rincome Hotel, and **Vanda Massage and Coffee Shop** on the seventh floor of the Muang Mai Hotel offer Thai massage of the world-famous variety.

GOLF

Enthusiasts can enjoy the fresh northern air on the 18-hole **Lanna Golf Course**, north of town on the Chotana Road, or on a nine-hole course at the **Gymkhana Club**.

EXPLORING BY MOTORBIKE

Motorbikes can be rented from many places, including **Pop's** at 53 Kotchasarn Road, ℂ (053) 236014 and **Daret's** (see above). The proprietor of the **Library Service** (see above) specializes in motorbike information.

TREKKING

For trekking, there are many organizations competing for your custom. We can recommend two, though this in no way implies that others are not as good or even better. The two following companies, though, are long-established and both insure their customers against mishaps. They are **Singha Travel Ltd,** ℂ (053) 233198; in Bangkok ℂ 2580160-5, and **Summit Tours and Trekking,** ℂ (053) 233351. Both are on the Tha Phae Road.

More locally, **Ox Cart Tours** will rumble you for the day beside paddy fields for 200 baht a person — ℂ (053) 222019.

FESTIVALS

Chiang Mai has one special festival of its own, the **FlowerFestival** which features floral floats and parades and lasts for three days from the first Friday in February.

In addition, Songkran and Yee Peng are observed, as elsewhere in the country. (See under Festivals in THE SIAMESE WORLD for details).

TOURIST INFORMATION

The new Chiang Mai **TAT Office** (ℂ (053) 248604-5) faces the river on the Chiang Mai — Lumphun Road (turn right immediately after crossing the Nawarat Bridge when coming from the Tha Phae Gate).

Mail

The Post Office is just by the railway station — look out for sign 'Chiangmai Satellite Earth Station Office'. It's open 8:30 to 4:30 weekdays (closed 12 to 1 for lunch), and 8:30 to 12 Saturday and Sunday. Overseas phone, fax and telex services are open 24 hours.

Chiang Mai – ABOVE: Wat Phra Singh;
OPPOSITE: Doi Suthep.

GETTING THERE

Thai Airways fly to Chiang Mai seven times a day from Bangkok. Economy class costs 1,335 baht at the time of writing. Ring them on ((053) 211044-7 for return reservations, or flights onwards to Chiang Rai or Mae Hong Son.

Chiang Mai is the terminus of the country's northern railway line. One daytime and four overnight trains make the

14-hour trip from Bangkok. They're comfortable, and there's a good restaurant car.

It's a long way to go by coach, but there are overnight coaches, from Bangkok's Northern Bus Station.

AROUND CHIANG MAI

Many of the most popular attractions are a few kilometers out of Chiang Mai.

On the road out to Doi Suthep the **Zoo** and the nearby **Arboretum** are small-scale but attractive. And, at the foot of the hill, the **Khru Ba Siwichai Statue**, erected in 1935 and commemorating the monk who

initiated the scheme to build the road up to Doi Suthep in 1934, is rarely without its devotees. The 11 km (seven miles) road was built by voluntary labor without any mechanical assistance. It was completed in an astonishing five months and 22 days, each village that contributed labor being responsible for no more than five meters (18 ft).

DOI SUTHEP

But it's **Wat Doi Suthep** itself that is the real attraction.

The temple (its official name is Wat Phra That Doi Suthep) was built in the fourteenth century to house a relic of the Buddha discovered near Sukhothai. The relic was brought to Chiang Mai and what is now known as Wat Suan Dok was built to house it. But one day it mysteriously divided in two, and so a new home had to be found for the new half. So a sacred white elephant was released. Followed by a band of eager monks, it made its way up onto the mountain, turned round three times and lay down. This was clearly the correct site for the new temple.

The startling position of the temple testifies to the perspicacity of elephants. Accompanied by numerous Thais, you climb over 300 steps, past musicians and blind beggars, from the car-park to the sacred precinct. Below you lies all of Chiang Mai, its airport almost at your feet. Wispy clouds threaten to interrupt the view, while behind you children run the length of ranks of holy bells, pushing each as they pass till it emits its sonorous tone into the still air. "Don't shake the bells" requests a sign.

The Buddha relic is contained in the golden *chedi* at the rear. The central part of the small space is occupied by the main temple building — you're not allowed into this wearing shorts.

Down in the car-park area again, hollyhocks bloom in the dry season and strawberries are on sale, both reminders of the temperate climates emulated by this part of the country.

A ROYAL PALACE

Ten kilometers (six miles) further up the road, the grounds of the **Royal Winter Palace** are open Fridays, weekends and public holidays except when members of the royal family are in residence (traditionally in January).

The gardens exude an almost English air. The benign and dignified Chiang Mai citizens move through the misty, rose-

scented coolness, with pines above and cloudlets below, in a double trance, posing for photos holding on to particularly gorgeous blooms, excelling even themselves in docility and dignified languor.

Four kilometers (three miles) further on again lies a **Meo village**, unfortunately much visited by tourists. But a few meters from the souvenir stalls there is a striking viewing-point with vistas out over hills covered with teak forests towards Burma.

ELEPHANT CAMPS

North of the city lie the elephant kraals. You can watch the magnificent crea-

tures washing in a small river, rolling and piling logs and taking visitors for short rides any morning at 9 am at the **Mae Sa Elephant Camp**, 10 km (6 miles) from town on Route 1096. Commercial and contrived it may sound, but the elephants at least are doing it for real. And with their huge, butterfly-wing ears and massive toenails, their penetrating eyes and cumbrous grace as they indulgently wallow in the stream or ingest whole hands of bananas, plastic

string included, they are true objects of wonder.

The same sort of thing can be seen on a rather larger scale at the **Chiang Dao Young Elephant Training Center**, 65 km (40 miles) north on Route 107. Here you can in addition take a look at the large **Chiang Dao Cave**, a few kilometers further on, in the same excursion. And on either trip, the **Sai Nam Phung Orchid Nursery** can also be included.

LUMPHUN

This town is reputed to be the oldest in Thailand, and its **Wat Jamathevi** and

Wat Prathard Haripoonchai, both little visited by Western tourists, each claim a thousand years of history. Lumphun is a half-hour's drive from Chiang Mai, and on the way there you can visit the partially reconstructed remains of the ancient city of **Wieng Goomgarn**.

SHOPPING FOR CRAFTS

For some reason, all the **Craft Centers** are out along the road to Borsang, running

silver are on show. You see the metal heated, hammered into shape, and then decorated with innumerable blows using sharp-pointed nails.

A little further on, on your right, is the **Shinawatra Thai Silk Factory,** ((053) 331959. Here girls work hand-looms with hand-operated flying shuttles as in the early days of the textile industry in Europe. Boys dye the silk by hand, and there are a few specimen silk-worms and an explanation of their life-cycle. What

straight out of the city to the east.

The pattern is usually the same. What you see is a small workshop where you can inspect the processes by which the product is created, and next to it is a far larger show-room where a wide variety of produce is on sale. So long as you don't believe all the material in the show-rooms was made in the workshops you are shown, you should find it an interesting experience.

There are several establishments dealing in the various crafts, silverware, silk, wood-carving and lacquerware. Near to the Super Highway, on your left leaving Chiang Mai, is **Lanna Thai**, ((053) 331-426, where the various stages of working

you learn here is that the worms are boiled to death when in the chrysalis stage to re-lease the silk hair with which they sought to protect themselves — a feature of the process that might put off some prospective customers.

Further on, down a lane to your left, is **Lanna Lacquerware**, ((053) 331606, a small family business where the wooden ducks, bowls and plates could easily have all been made on the premises.

Northern crafts – LEFT: Silk umbrellas from the "umbrella village" of Borsang; ABOVE: hilltribe products — dolls made by the Meo tribe on sale in Chiang Mai.

Wood-carving, as well as various kinds of weaving, can be seen at the **Hilltribe Handicrafts Center,** ((053) 331977.

BORSANG — UMBRELLA VILLAGE

All of this commercial activity comes to a head in the village of **Borsang** itself where the main street consists entirely of shops aimed at the tourist. The speciality here, though, is umbrella-making, and Borsang's hand-painted umbrellas, whether made of paper or cloth, are famous round the world.

One of the smaller workshops is **Suwan House** where carved teak furniture is also made. The heavy tables, with scenes of rustic life deeply cut into the table-tops, and every available inch decorated in some way, are very beautiful. Each table, together with its eight chairs, takes two men six months to make. The prices are reasonable, but the cost of shipping these bulky items to Europe or America more than doubles the sum would-be exporters have to reckon on.

When in Borsang, no-one should miss **Wat Bauk Pet**, a kilometer further along the side-road that constitutes the village's main street. A brand-new temple has been constructed next to the older building, with a striking mural of massed monks on the wall facing the road. Inside, the ceiling is on object-lesson in the deceptive arts of *trompe l'oeil,* while celestial elephants, pink and emerald lotuses, reclining matrons and green-bodied gods crowd the walls.

This kind of Indian-inspired Thai art perfectly exemplifies the national belief in the virtue of brilliance and intensity, and the general Asian preference for the gorgeous and the new as opposed to the faded and old, however venerable.

MAE HONG SON

The best way to get to this remote hill town is by the half-hour flight from Chiang Mai.

The alternative is an eight-hour coach journey by Highway 108, soon to be reduced to four hours when a new road to the north, via Pai, is completed.

A BIRD'S EYE VIEW

The flight from Chiang Mai shows how uninhabited vast tracts of upland northern Thailand are. Wooded hills succeed each other as far as the eye can see, with a very occasional tiny patch of cultivation visible in the river valleys.

Mae Hong Son is a delightful place. As soon as you get out of the little plane, you are aware of the quiet, the dry air and the pastoral relaxation.

The town occupies a rare flat area in the valley of the River Pai. It's small and for the most part built of wooden houses. The population is only six thousand or so, plus the few dozen hill-tribe people who come down in the cold early mornings to the market. Hondas and the occasional pickup truck try to give the place a touch of bustle, but they don't succeed. Boys play football on the airport runway after the last flight of the day has left, and a couple of miles out of town you're in a world of buffalo carts trundling along empty roads that wind through undramatic but most attractive hill scenery.

Tourism has in fact only recently arrived here. As recently as the early eighties the high level of Communist guerilla activity led to an official policy of discouraging foreigners from visiting the district. Now the only danger is from the occasional bandit — something visitors should be aware of, but not allow to spoil their stay in this very special landscape.

WHERE TO STAY

The **Maetee Hotel** ((053) 611141; 39 rooms; rates: inexpensive) is a typical provincial small-town hotel, simple but clean, conveniently situated right in the

Chiang Mai — Buddhas on the altar of Wat Phra Singh.

center of town, and with the advantage of being patronized mostly by Thais. The **Siam Hotel** (☎ (053) 611148; 14 rooms; rates: inexpensive) is similar. A third hotel of the same kind, the **Baiyoke** (☎ (053) 611486; rates: inexpensive) is opposite the Post Office. There are in addition a number of extremely cheap guest-houses off the main street and down by the lake.

For more up-market accommodation you have to go a few kilometers out of

town. The **Rim Nam Klang Doi Resort** (☎ (053) 611086; 16 rooms; rates: moderate) is a very attractive place. There's a restaurant and bungalows dotted about on the banks of the Pai. Campers are welcome (tents are provided), and there's also inexpensive accommodation available in a dormitory.

The **Mae Hong Son Resort** (☎ (053) 611504; 27 rooms; rates: moderate) is similar in arrangement, but the rooms are rather more luxurious, and the place makes further gestures towards being the top people's choice by providing a cocktail lounge and a souvenir shop. Even so, it too offers cheap dormitory accommoda-

tion. Again, it's right on the banks of the river.

ABOUT TOWN

After Dark
There isn't a lot to do after sunset, and people generally go to bed early. The **Bua Tong Restaurant,** ☎ (053) 611187, is the best in a town where it's impossible to spend more than US$3-4 on a meal. It serves good local food in attractive wooden surroundings. Mae Hong Son's night life, such as it is, is centered on the **Sunny Coffee Shop**.

Two Temples
The town itself has two main attractions — a small and picturesque lake, overlooked by a temple with a corrugated-iron roof, and a second and more substantial temple spectacularly situated on top of a hill.

Turn left at the Post Office to get to the lake-side **Wat Chong Klang**. It's brilliantly colored, like all Thai temples, and houses paintings on glass brought from Burma in the last century.

To reach the hill-top **Wat Phra That Doi Kong Mu**, from the crossroads outside the Maetee Hotel take the road opposite the hotel entrance, past the red post box. This will lead you to a colorful roadside monastery, **Wat Phra Non**. The road goes up just to the left of the monastery and is a 20 minute walk. An alternative for the sturdy is to walk up through the monastery, pass between two stone lions, and scramble up the steep track direct to the summit temple complex. There were once steps here but they have been for the most part buried in mud (baked earth in the dry season). This route will get you to the top, hot and very thirsty, in little more than ten minutes.

The view over Mae Hong Son and the surrounding hills is wonderful. The smallness of the town and the vast silence of the countryside is very beautiful.

TREKKING

There are a number of advertisements for treks and one-day outings displayed outside establishments along the length of the main street, but they're almost all for the same tours. Working elephants lumber up these wooded hills, and bamboo rafts (or boats) will transport you downriver, just as they will in the more frequented country around Chiang Mai.

south of the town is unlikely to be enjoyable — there're only four of them, and they're virtual, if not actual, prisoners, held specifically to be "exhibited" — for a price — to tourists.

OUT OF TOWN

The country around Mae Hong Son consists of wooded, steep-sided hills between which vigorous rivers run. It is wholly unspoilt, either by tourism or in-

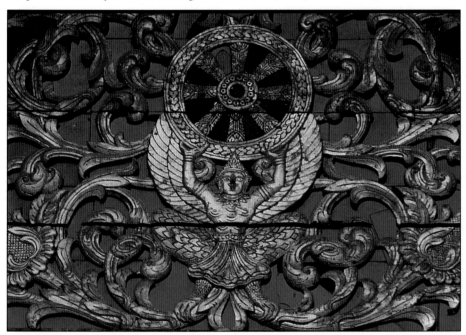

The difference is that there are fewer tourists in this region, and that Mae Hong Son itself is such a delightfully restful place in which to be based.

Of the agents themselves, **Khun Trading, (** (053) 611303, appear reliable, as do the owners of the Bua Tong Restaurant (see above) who operate two- and three-day tours under the name **Central Tour**.

The trips themselves are the usual mix — expeditions by truck, boat and on foot taking in a number of hill-tribe villages. Most include a short section riding on an elephant — this, though, is expensive and can double the price of a one-day trip. Only the visit to the "long-necked women" (Karens)

dustry. Houses are almost invariably built of wood, and many are roofed with large leaves.

One of the nicest things to do is to hire a motorbike and head off into the countryside. Anyone renting you out a bike will give you a sketch-map of the district and suggest routes that take in points of interest and keep to the more reasonable roads. A sturdy little Honda Dream will take you to many of the places you will want to visit.

There's only the one modern road, and it follows the valley without staying close to

OPPOSITE and ABOVE: Highly-wrought gilded metalwork in Chiangmai temples.

the river. Both north and south of the town are fascinating.

To the north, the road winds easily beneath cliffs until, after seven kilometers (four miles), it crosses the Pai by a solid modern bridge. It then rises to give some fine views, descending again after another 11 km (7 miles) to the valley floor of a tributary of the main river.

The Fish Cave

Called in Thai "Tham Pla", this small rec-

reation area is clearly marked on the left of the road. It isn't, on the surface, much to write home about, yet it has a touch of true innocence, and a lot of genuine charm.

Its name derives from a place where a stream emerges from under a cliff and large blue carp can be seen down through a hole in the rock, circling in wait for visitors' tit-bits.

In itself it's unspectacular, but the adjacent area has been turned into an attrac-

tive water-side garden with lilies, a large water-wheel, and tables and chairs set out under the trees. It's the work of a National Park — not surprisingly, as they're responsible for the excellent management of beauty spots all over the country. Food and drink are available near the entrance.

A Forest Park

A few yards back up the road before the Fish Cave, an unpaved road leads off left — coming from Mae Hong Son — towards a waterfall (seven kilometers, four miles) in a Forest Park. The road is good for the first three kilometers (two miles), as far as a village, but then deteriorates as it begins to climb. Motorcyclists have found the way difficult — organized trips from Mae Hong Son in four-wheel drive vehicles go there most days.

Southwards

The countryside is less striking to begin with south of the town, though there's an attractive un-made up road that runs past the Rim Nam Klang Doi and Mae Hong Son resorts, between the main road and the river.

After 12 km (7 miles) you come to the **Hot Springs** at **Pha Bong**. These are not worth visiting. It looks as if an attempt has been made to landscape the area around where the very hot and foul-smelling sulphurous water emerges, but clearly enthusiasm quickly waned.

After Pha Bong you can either follow the road where it climbs a long and rather steep hill, or you can turn off to the left down a track, almost immediately after the village, and visit the **dam** across the Mae Ra Mat River.

If you stay on the main road, after a few kilometers you'll come, at the top of first long hill, to a clearly marked **Scenic Area** on the left. This has an excellent view of the valley below, and of the dam across a side-valley a couple of kilometers away straight ahead, with distant mountains behind it.

OPPOSITE: Pastoral cool by the Kok River. Northern Thailand consists of agricultural land following the rivers as they wind through forested hill country. ABOVE: Chiang Mai's Wat Suan Dok.

THE FAR NORTH

CHIANG RAI

Situated on the banks of the Kok River, Chiang Rai is the gateway to the far north. It has sometimes been denigrated as a place with little to recommend it, but with its wide main street and good hotels, its very pleasant Thai restaurant and fresh climate, Chiang Rai is no bad place to

Wangcome (℃ (053) 711800; fax: 713844; 221 rooms; rates: moderate), a luxury hotel with remarkably reasonable room rates. Now there is another top-class establishment — but it's also top-priced. This is the **Dusit Island Resort** (℃ (053) 715989-997; fax: 715988; rates: expensive), situated on a small island in the Kok River. The **Wiang Inn** (℃ (053) 711533; fax: 711877; 260 rooms; rates: moderate) is also both comfortable and reasonable.

spend a day at the beginning and end of any tour of this border region, or to use as a base for day-long excursions.

Getting There

You can fly to Chiang Rai from Chiang Mai — the three daily flights connect with the ones coming up to Chiang Mai from Bangkok. Flight time is 40 minutes.

Most people, though, take the bus. The three and a half hour trip up the H1019 road is relatively painless, with a short stop for refreshments at Ban Mae Kachan.

Where to Stay

The best hotel in town used to be the

Restaurants etc.

Apart from the hotels, the best place to eat is the moderately-priced **Hownaliga Restaurant,** ℃ (053) 711062. Sporting a choice turn of phrase — "We welcome to service you" — it's centrally situated on the Banparrakarn Road. German food is available at the open-air **Bierstube**, close to the Wangcome.

Chiang Rai's night-life centers on the Wangcome's **Music Room**; there is also a little place directly opposite called the **Thala Cafe**.

What to See

Chiang Rai is the setting-off point for

many river trips to visit the hill tribes and the landing-stage, opposite the island, is a photogenic place worth a visit even if you're proceeding north or west by other means. Otherwise a much-venerated statue and two temples are all that need detain you.

Chiang Rai was once the capital of the independent Lanna kingdom, only becoming Thai territory in 1786 after having been under Burmese control. The **Monument to King Mengrai** at the intersection of Uttakit Road and Singhakai Road commemorates the town's thirteenth century founder and is rarely without its incense-burning and flower-laying devotees.

Wat Phrasingh and **Wat Phra Keo**, the latter distinguished by once having been home to Bangkok's celebrated Emerald Buddha, are each worth a quick look.

Trekking

A number of establishments in Chiang Rai offer treks to visit hill-tribes. Among these are the **Chiang Rai Travel and Tour Company,** ((053) 713314; telex as for the Wangcome Hotel, and the **Chiang Rai Travel Information Center** ((053) 711-062. It has to be mentioned that there have been armed attacks on river boats carrying tourists on the Kok River, with passengers and boatmen killed. Armed police patrols to accompany the boats are being instituted at the time of writing, but it would be as well, at the very least, to check the current situation locally before making any bookings.

It's safer to travel by unpretentious public bus. It's the tourists' money bandits are after, and the humble local vehicles are rarely held up. They may, of course, become over-loaded and crash into the river, drowning all occupants. The answer here is simply to get off and wait for the next one if the bus seems really very full and the driver quite unusually reckless.

Northern markets are characterized by the freshness of their produce and the greater variety afforded by the upland climate. This market is Chiang Rai's.

CHIANG SAEN

Fifty-nine kilometers (37 miles) from Chiang Rai, this riverside town is quite simply the nicest little place imaginable. Sited on the bank of the broad Mekong river, with views across its waters to Laos, Chiang Saen, now hardly more than a village, has a placidity and charm that expresses all the ease and geniality that life in Laos used not so long ago to be famous for.

Chedis crumble in a swirl of morning glory, and hollyhocks and roses bloom smilingly round the temples. Along the waterfront, stall-holders sell fruit on wooden balconies high out above the stream, while over on the Lao shore flame-of-the-forest trees blossom an astonishingly luminous scarlet.

The Great River

Laos-watching is Chiang Saen's distinctive pleasure. The Mekong is very wide, but people can be clearly seen, girls bathing, monks strolling, and children playing with a dog. Buffaloes roam at will along the shore.

It is the presence of the Mekong that makes Chiang Saen so magical. The brown surface of the river is luminous in the heat, and there is ample space for both countries to ply their water-borne trade along their respective channels. It's one of the world's great rivers, and, with its combined docility and strength, and a summery haze over the distant reaches, its beauty entirely envelops the little town.

A Long History

The origins of this ancient settlement are lost in the celebrated mists of antiquity, mists that gather rather more readily in this part of the world than elsewhere. But even before the town's refounding in 1328 by a grandson of Chiang Rai's King Mengrai it was almost certainly an important place. Its northerly situation, however, meant it became an inevitable victim of Thai-Burmese rivalry. The Burmese successfully seized

the city in 1558, the Thais retaking it in the early nineteenth century, sacking it in the process.

At the end of the century, however, King Chulalongkorn, the great restorer of things lost, had descendants of the former residents sought out and brought back to the site. The place has thrived, albeit in a modest way, ever since.

What to See
One kilometer before you get to the river, on your right, stands the **Museum**. It contains a small collection of Buddhas and stone-carvings and is open from 9 am to 4 pm, Wednesdays to Sundays (closed Mondays, Tuesdays and public holidays. You may also find it shut between 1 and 2 pm).

The temples of Chiang Saen are picturesque but not of major importance. The most striking temple in the immediate area is **Wat Phra That a-Kgao**, dramatically sited on a hill-top south of the town, four kilometers (three miles) along the road to Chiang Khong.

Where to Eat
An essential item in any visit to Chiang Saen is a meal at the **Sala Thai Restaurant**. It's situated at the T-junction where the road from Chiang Rai meets the river. As far as roads go, all Chiang Saen is a T-junction, and the Sala Thai is at its very heart. You're right on the river, and you can gaze across at Laos over a bottle of Kloster while the excellent sour chicken soup is being prepared. It's one of the nicest places in Thailand, but unfortunately not unknown to the coach-tour operators.

Where to Stay
There are several small guest-houses in Chiang Saen. The **Lanna Guest House** (10 rooms; rates: inexpensive) on the river is recommended, while the imposing-look-

The Kok River runs down to Chiang Rai from wild border country close to the Burmese frontier. Treks up-river from Chiang Rai tend to appeal to the more daring travelers.

ing **Poonsuk Hotel** (10 rooms; rates: inexpensive), on your right as you approach the river, just before the Sala Thai Restaurant, is actually rather basic.

THE GOLDEN TRIANGLE

This is an evocative phrase suggesting both legends and an arcane mystery. What it actually means here on the borders of Burma, Laos and Thailand is a rather large area of land, shaped roughly like a trian-

venir stalls along the top of a 10 m (33 ft) high river bank. What they overlook, and what all the fuss is purportedly about, is a perfectly flat, treeless, shrubless island the size of a small sports stadium that an increase of a couple of meters in river level would immediately innundate.

Its interest is that it belongs to none of the three countries. Somebody cultivates it, however, as it is neatly raked over and shows signs of a green crop — lettuces, someone said, for the tourist restaurants

gle with its long base south of Chiang Mai and its apex somewhere in Burma, where the majority of the world's opium crop is grown.

But the colorful words have proved too good a tourist magnet to be resisted, and it's hard to market an ill-defined area of land stretching over international borders. Hence a specific location had to be promoted as the legendary triangle itself. The point where, at the confluence of the Sop Ruak and Mekong rivers, Thailand, Laos and Burma meet was the inevitable choice.

This Golden Triangle, then, is a joke. What you see when you arrive at the village, **Sop Ruak**, is a fairground of sou-

here on the Thai bank. There is no sign of any interest in the spot by either of the other two countries.

A Viewing Point

Even so, the river scene is on a grand enough scale to be beautiful despite the tourists. The best place to view it is a small hill, close to where all the coaches park, where there's a pavilion attached to a monastery, **Wat Phra Thai Pukhao.**

Accommodation

At the time of writing two new luxury resorts are poised to take advantage of this bizarre spot's reputation — the **Baan Boran**

Hotel (€ in Bangkok 2514707, fax: 254-5753), managed by the same company as the Phuket Yacht Club, and the **Golden Triangle Resort Hotel** (€ (053) 713354; fax: 714170; 74 rooms; rates: expensive). Things, it seems, are all set to change in this once remote corner of the country.

How to Get There
You can get to Sop Ruak from Chiang Saen on an extraordinary vehicle, a four-seater motorbike-bus. It's an enlarged version of the pedicab, and it bumps along the rough 11 km (7 miles) road — which keeps to the bank of the Mekong — sporting a child's pink plastic windmill whirring on the front handlebars.

MAE SAI

Once you reach Mae Sai, you really are at the end of the road. It continues on across a bridge into Burma, but foreigners other than Thais are not allowed to enter Burma by this route.

Mae Sai is a shabby, dusty town that feels more Burmese than Thai. The frontier, anyway, is merely a stream children have no trouble kicking a football over, and during daylight hours a throng jostles busily in each direction over the border bridge.

Still, with hill-tribe children in costume posing for photos against the border signposts — 5 baht a shot is the usual fee they ask with the only English words they know — and mounds of strawberries on sale throughout the dry months, the place does have a character all of its own.

The strawberries achieve the status of a cult at the height of the season, in mid-February. They are on sale everywhere, not only in the town but also from stalls along the main road, together with bottles of lethal-looking strawberry juice. There is even a Strawberry Festival in Mae Sai, with processions, brass bands and a beauty contest. Check with TAT in Chiang Mai or Bangkok for the dates.

Over the frontier stream is hilly country, and Burma peers down on Mae Sai, its

lights and fires flickering in the cold nights. For a view of the town, the river and Burma beyond, climb the 206 steps that ascend to a *chedi* on a hilltop from **Wat Phra That Doi Wao** in the center of town.

Where to Stay
There are plenty of places to stay in the town, but they vary a lot in the value they offer. The good places are reasonable enough, but the bad are really very bad indeed.

There are two very new, clean hotels on the main street, the **Sin Watana** (€ (053) 731950; 30 rooms; rates: moderate) and the **Tai Tong** (€ (053) 731560; 14 rooms; rates: moderate). There are several bungalow hotels down by the river — of these, the **Northern Guest House** (€ (053) 731537; 30 rooms; rates: inexpensive) is acceptable if you take their best, rather than their cheapest, rooms.

A Gigantic Cave
For the **King's Cave**, turn left off the main road five kilometers (three miles) before Mae Sai at a prominent sign. Two and a half kilometers along a side-road you come to the entrance. Drinks, and strawberries in season, are on sale, and you can hire a flashlight for 15 baht.

The cave extends an astonishing seven kilometers (four miles) into the limestone mountain. In the rainy season, only the first 500 m (1/3 mile) is accessible. This first section, though, gives a good idea of the cave's general character. The way is always roomy and never cramped. The floor is sandy — where it becomes rocky, concrete steps have been built. The usual limestone cave characteristics, stalactites, stalagmites and "rock fountains" can be seen.

The second 500 m is even easier than the first, but after that the route becomes very difficult. Thus a kilometer (2/3 mile) is as far as the ordinary visitor can go.

There is something very special about Chiang Saen. As a modern town it's insignificant, but its extensive ruins surrounded by tenuous contemporary economic activity on the banks of the Mekong give it a rare poignancy.

DOI THUNG

This mountain of 2,000 m (6,600 ft) with a temple, Phra That Doi Tung, on the summit, is a popular destination with local people. Get off the Chiang Rai — Mae Sai bus at **Huai Khrai**, 19 km (12 miles) before Mae Sai, and from where the bus puts you down minibuses leave up the hill road. The fare to Doi Thung from here is 30 baht.

The wind sounds in the pine trees and bells of various sizes tinkle. The buildings were rebuilt in 1973 and are not spectacular, but the location is magnificent and the views, when free of cloud, splendid.

The temple is much revered because it contains remains of the Lord Buddha. The road up is metalled all the way. You pass half a dozen hill-tribe villages en route, Akha and Lahu. The **Akha Guest House**, on your left on the way up, has 12 inexpensive rooms and a restaurant, but if you're thinking of staying, take a mosquito net as none are provided. The former Doi Tung Guest House is no longer in business.

The Doi Thung area is in the process of becoming a major resources development district, with the aim primarily reforestation. The project is linked to a palace and health-center being built for the Thai Princess Mother.

MAE SALONG

This is the mountain village close to the Burmese border settled by a group of Chinese Kuomintang refugees.

From **Mae Chan**, a small town 28 km (17 miles) north of Chiang Rai, take the road for Mae Sai, and after two kilometers turn off at a sign on the left to the Hill-tribe Development Center and Mae Salong.

After 12 km (seven miles) you reach the **Hill-tribe Center**, a large establishment employing 200 people in the attempt to show the hill-tribes a more enlightened way of life than growing opium poppies in temporary forest clearings.

Another 24 km (15 miles) and a good climb further on is Mae Salong, settled by a group of Chinese Nationalists after their defeat by the Communists in China in 1949. The views, and the flowers in season, are magnificent, though the houses with their corrugated-iron roofs are less impressive. But it's a unique place, neither Thai nor hill-tribe, the home of people stranded by history in wild frontier territory.

Should you want to stay there, there's accommodation at the **Mae Salong Resort** (Telephone and fax: ((053) 714047) and elsewhere.

A NOTE ON THE HILL TRIBES

The following information is extracted from the booklet *The Hill Tribes of Thailand*, published by the Technical Service Club Tribal Research Institute in Bangkok.

Evidence of language puts the hill tribes into two groups, one originating from the Tibetan plateau, the other more locally. In the former, Sino-Tibetan, group are the Karen, Meo, Yao, Lahu, Lisu and Akha tribes. In the latter, Austro-Asiatic, group are the Lua, H'tin, Khamu and Mlabri tribes.

The agricultural practices of the tribes vary, but it's the tribes that practise shifting cultivation — moving on to another patch of land when one has been temporarily exhausted — that cause the problems to the authorities. Not only is it these people who cultivate opium (which, incidentally, only grows well at altitudes

MEO, or **H'MONG**   A people widespread in southern China, they trace kinship through the father and the men can have more than one wife. They live at high altitudes, and are more extensively engaged in opium production than any other hill tribe.

LAHU   This tribe lives only at high altitudes, is monogamous, and cultivates opium among other crops in slash-and-burn agriculture. Though they worship their ancestors, they believe in a single god called Geushu.

of 1,000 m — 3,280 ft — and over) but their slash-and-burn methods are leading to extensive deforestation in the northern hills.

See A LIFE IN THE HILLS in the SIAMESE WORLD section for more on the hill tribe question. If you're interested in buying hill tribe crafts, see the Hilltribe Handicrafts Center in Chiang Mai (p. 165).

KAREN   Far and away the largest tribe, these people largely occupy areas close to the Burmese border. They are happy to live at a lower altitude, are monogamous, trace kinship through the mother, and have adopted opium recently rather than cultivating it as a traditional crop.

YAO   Cultivating dry rice and corn, these people are polygamous, and the adoption of children is common. They show great influence of Chinese culture, and popular Taoism has influenced their religion.

AKHA   Thought to have arrived in Thailand in the 1880s, they are shifting cultivators, monogamous, with complex rituals associated with spirit propitiation and ancestor worship.

ABOVE: Akha men pursuing their life of ease on a remote road in the north. Despite their insistent cultivation of the opium poppy, the relaxed and amused life of the hilltribes adds an incomparable air of charm to northern life. OPPOSITE: a poppy head is cut to extract the potent sap.

LISU Subdivided into the Flowery Lisu and the Black Lisu, they engage in shifting cultivation at around 1,000 m (3,280 ft) and grow opium for sale. They have strong social cohesion and have a reputation as individualists.

LUA Unlike the other tribes, the Lua are found only in Northern Thailand and have largely been absorbed into Thai society. Those remaining in the hills have the reputation of being conservation-minded.

KHAMU These are a small group found mainly in Nan Province. They are part cultivators, part hunters. Their shamans are very highly regarded as religio-magical practitioners in Laos.

HTIN This tribe consists of migratory slash-and-burn farmers and is only found in Nan Province. They are animists, though some villages have Buddhist temples.

MLABRI This tiny group, numbering only about 150, are hunter-gatherers. They have no fixed settlements and move their camp-site every three or four days.

Hilltribe girls – ABOVE: Akha; OPPOSITE: Yao.

Off the
Beaten
Track

For anyone intent on discovering "new" palm-fringed islands, Thailand's southwest is its last frontier. It's lightly populated, entirely rural, and the coast is scattered with what are still for the most part untouristed islands.

How much longer this will remain so is anyone's guess, but if Thai tourism continues to expand at the current rate it won't be very long. The situation at present is rather like that in Greece in the 'sixties and 'seventies — every season the spotlight falls on a new island, and what begins as "undiscovered" very quickly becomes the name that's on everyone's lips. Needless to say, the locals waste no time in erecting the necessary facilities to channel the unforeseen wealth that is suddenly coming their way — if, that is, the big commercial concerns don't get in there before them.

Nevertheless, the three southwestern provinces of Krabi, Trang and Satun contain a wealth of peace and simple pleasure.

KOH JUM

Thirty-five kilometers (22 miles) from Krabi Town and on the way out to Phi Phi Island is **Koh Jum**. This in-shore island is very like the others in this area, featuring limestone caves and coral reefs, with fine views of high marine stacks. The difference is Jum boasts a small bungalow hotel, **Jum Island Resort** (40 rooms; rates: inexpensive; bookings via Krabi ((075) 611541). A boat leaves Krabi for Jum every morning at 9 am, returning every afternoon. You can also get there from Laem Gruad to the south.

TRANG TOWN

Trang, 864 km (540 miles) south of Bangkok, is a very typical Thai provincial town, with few Western visitors in evidence. It is larger and considerably more attractive than Krabi. It's 25 km (16 miles) from the coast. Trang has, however, one superb new hotel, and is clearly gearing up to handle a whole new wave of tourism in the 1990s, and in the meantime is hosting all kinds of media events to draw attention to its charms.

The elegant, but remarkably inexpensive, new hostelry is the **Thumrin** (((075) 211011; 120 rooms; rates: moderate, but with average and above suites; telex: 72387 BKKACME TH), close to the station. There is also an older and rather basic hotel, the **Queen's** ((218229; 48 rooms; rates: inexpensive).

Trang has two parks, the **Praya Rasadanupradit Monument Park** and the **Sa Kapangsurin Park**, each only a kilometer west from the town center. The latter features a small lake.

Trang Airport (((075) 218224) is a small affair, but there's a morning flight every day to Bangkok, returning in the afternoon. All flights go via Phuket. The number for Thai Airways in Trang is ((075) 218066.

There is also a **railway station**, on a branch line that leaves the main line at Tung Song (half way between Surat Thani and Hat Yai) and runs down to the coast at Kantang. For the station, phone ((075) 218012.

Trang has an autumn **Vegetarian Festival**. Like Phuket's, its dates are fixed according to the lunar calendar, but fall sometime in late September or early October.

There is a **Tourist Service Center** at the Police Station, ((075) 218019, ext 191, and there are several travel agents on Thanon Wisatekoon.

TRANG PROVINCE

This quiet region offers the usual southwest Thailand mix — open country rising to low mountains inland, limestone caves and hot-water springs, and a largely untouched coast featuring spectacular rock

Going places — A "motorbike-bus" (see under THE GOLDEN TRIANGLE – HOW TO GET THERE), an enlarged and mechanised version of the traditional pedicab.

formations, exceptionally clear water, and innumerable sandy beaches.

Haad Pak Meng is the most accessible beach from the provincial capital, some 35 km (24 miles) to the west. The beach is 5 km (3 miles) long and faces out towards the extraordinary profile of precipitous Koh Meng. Backed with pine trees, it's a popular beach with campers.

A long-tailed boat can be hired at Pak Meng to take you the 30 minute trip to **Koh Hai**. The island is five square kilometers

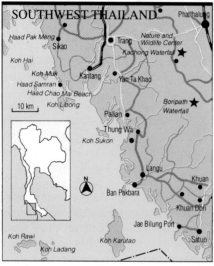

in size and currently has one hotel complex with a restaurant and 14 bungalows. Excellent coral reefs extend for two kilometers (just over a mile) about 400 m (1/4 mile) from the shore.

Kantang

The harbor, 25 km (16 miles) from Trang town, where boats can be found going to most of the province's off-shore islands, it's the end of the branch rail line and a small commercial port. Otherwise there's nothing to see there except the remains of a country residence of King Rama VI, **Tamnak Jan**. Set on a hill, it's now part of a public park.

Koh Libong

The largest island off the Trang coast, it has three villages, a headland (Cape Juhoi)

famous for its migrant birds and now a protected zone, and a long west-facing beach, Haad Thungyaka. Ornithologists are offered free accommodation — enquire at the Tourist Service Center in Trang town. Boats leave for Koh Libong from Kantang.

A Choice of Islands

Slightly further afield is **Koh Kradan**, often called Trang's most beautiful island. There's commercial rubber and coconut cultivation on the island, and accommodation is available.

Further south, lying 10 km (7 miles) off the coast of the sub-district of Palian, are **Koh Lao Lieng** and **Koh Petra** with their rich sub-marine life and swallows' nests. Nearer inland is the larger **Koh Sukon** (also known as *Koh Moo*. Inhabited mostly by Thai Muslims, the island has many good beaches and is famous for the quality of its water melons.

Mainland beaches

Back on the mainland, there are beaches at **Haad San**, **Haad Yong Ling**, and **Haad Chao Mai**, this last also featuring a cave. These are all in the area west of Kantang. Further south, and 49 km (33 miles) from Trang town, there is **Haad Samran** beach, backed by thick pine woods. And close to the small town of Palian, there is **Hyong-star Cape**, a local beauty spot.

Inland

Trang Province boasts a number of waterfalls, as well as caves bearing either the usual royal initials cut into the rock or sweetly smiling reclining Buddhas. You can see an example of the latter at **Wat Tham Soratpradit** (locally known as *Wat Tham Iso*) to the right of the main road running north out of Trang, just before you reach Huai Yot.

The waterfalls are all in the upland area to the east of Trang town. The nearest to the Trang to Had Yai road is the **Kachong Waterfall**, 20 km (13 miles) east of Trang. Near the waterfall there is also a small

Nature and Wildlife Center. A number of initials commemorating royal visits are carved on a large stone.

Before you reach Kachong there is a swampy lake known for its teal — look out for a sign on the right of the road to **Noknam Khlong Lamchan Park**.

A Waterfall Tour Route links a number of waterfalls south of Kachong in the **Mount Banthat** area, ending up on the Palian to Sathun Road, not far from Palian. It's a sound route for vehicles.

KOH TARU TAO

This is the main island of a group of 51 forming the Taru Tao Marine National Park. Limited accommodation is available from the Park authorities (16 rooms; reservations in Bangkok, (5790529). There's also provision for camping. Access to the island — 25 km (17 miles) off the coast — is from Pak Bara Pier, near La-gnoo, halfway between Palian and Satun. Weekend

Near the **Chaopha Waterfall** at the southern end of this trail you might be able to meet members of the Sakai, a migrant tribe of the Mount Banthat region.

Bullfighting

This is a popular entertainment in southern Thailand generally. It is totally unlike the Spanish variety — instead it's a test of strength between two bulls. Fights usually take place on Sunday afternoons, and are worth catching if you get the chance.

trips can be booked from travel agents in Hat Yai during the dry season.

Forty kilometers (25 miles) west of Koh Taru Tao is the island cluster of **Adang-Rawi**. Basic accommodation is available on Koh Adang.

THE NORTHEAST

Invariably known as "Esarn" by Thais, after the pre-Angkor kingdom that flourished in this area and in neighboring Cambodia, the northeast is Thailand's despised, rejected, neglected and almost forgotten region.

The tranquility of Thailand's far south – skies shine, a fish jumps, the heat reflects off the surface of the water.

Esarn is an upland plain, a vast rice-growing plateau constantly under threat of drought. If the monsoon is inadequate, poverty, with its attendant horrors of starvation and disease, quickly slips into its accustomed place.

This is the part of Thailand where leprosy continues to elude the underfunded attempts of the authorities to stamp it out, where in desperation the people take to masquerading as monks and nuns to become "false-beggars", and where the hunting of toads to sell to the manufacturers of wallets and handbags for one baht per four animals is common.

Yet this huge area is, despite everything, routinely considered by Thais as the "real" Thailand. Here Westernization has had least effect (except during the Vietnam War when the Americans set up three huge bases there). Very few tourists visit the Great Plain, but if you're keen to get away from other foreigners, and don't mind the lack of Western comforts, this could well be the direction in which to head.

The area has strong links with Laos to the east. Lao, or a Thai dialect very close to it, though looked down on elsewhere in the country, is the true language of the region. The historical remains and art here tend to be Khmer rather than Thai.

Getting There

This presents no problems. You can fly from Bangkok to Udon Thani, Ubon Ratchathani, Khon Kaen or Sakon Nakhon, and there are overnight trains from Bangkok north to Udon Thani and Nong Khai, and east to Khorat (Nakhon Ratchasima), Buri Ram, Surin and Ubon Ratchathani.

The main route through the region is the road running north from Bangkok to Udon Thani. It's essentially the communications link between Bangkok and Vientiane, the Lao capital, but relations between the two countries are rarely good enough to allow it to serve its true function.

OPPOSITE: Tobacco harvest.

PHIMAI

Nakhon Ratchasima, usually known as "Khorat", is reckoned sufficiently important to merit a TAT office, the only one in the region. The reason for this is no doubt the twelfth century Khmer ruins at **Phimai**, 60 km (37 miles) further along the road — there's also a small museum attached. Nakhon Ratchasima is remarkably prosperous, and the young citizens parading its central square in the early evening quite as elegant as their Bangkok counterparts. The best hotel is the **Chomsurang** (((044) 257088-9; 119 rooms; rates: moderate).

PHANOM RUNG

Standing magnificently on a hilltop near **Burirum**, these remarkably intact Khmer remains are, like Phimai, a fortress and temple in one. Phanom Rung is much visited by Thais on account of a carved lintel, recovered from the U.S.A. in 1988 after much diplomatic activity. It had allegedly been smuggled out of Thailand, and its return was a source of considerable national pride.

UDON THANI

This important city close to the border with Laos is a good base from which to explore the region. Despite the fact that it has no taxis in the normal sense, and transport within the city is by pedal-powered *samlor,* Udon has all the appearance of being a prosperous place. Its new park, **Nong Phra Jak**, and clean, wide streets testify to far-sighted local government policies.

The best hotel, the **Charoen** (((042) 248155; fax: 246126; 120 rooms; rates: moderate), has a sophisticated restaurant and a rather basic swimming-pool. Air-conditioned rooms are also available at the **Charoensri Palace** (((042) 242611-3; fax: 222601; 70 rooms; rates: moderate), the **Udon Hotel** (((042) 246528-30; fax: 242782; 100 rooms; rates: moderate), and the **Siriudorn** (℃ (042) 222331-2; 98 rooms; rates: inexpensive).

There are attractive outdoor restaurants overlooking the park — the fashionable **Rabieng Patchanee** (℃ (042) 241-515) can be recommended. Slightly further out of town, **T-J's Restaurant** (℃ (042) 247293) specialises in Western food.

BAN CHIANG

This archaeological site (closed Mondays and Tuesdays) makes a convenient half-day trip out of Udon Thani — take one of the frequent buses that leave for Sakhon Nakon from 100 m to your right coming out of the Chareon Hotel, and after 50 km (32 miles) get off at the junction for Ban Chiang. Motorbike-buses wait to take you the four kilometers (two and a half miles) to the site (fare between 20 and 70 baht — a real bargaining situation).

Artefacts found here show that between 3,600 BC and AD 200 there existed in this region an advanced civilization whose accomplishments included the making of bronze and iron tools and utensils, pottery and glass beads, weaving, and the cultivation of rice. The implication is that metallurgical technology was not imported from India or China, as had previously been thought, but was evolved here independently, and earlier.

Entrance to the **Museum** is 10 baht. It is of an international standard and very informative — Ban Chiang is a major site and was excavated between 1972 and 1975 with the help of the University of Pennsylvania.

At another site, half a mile to the left on coming out of the museum, an actual excavation site is preserved, with some objects in place, in the grounds of a temple. Produce your museum admission ticket and there is no further charge.

NONG KHAI

Buses leave Udon Thani for Nong Khai from the New Bus Station; the fare is 15 baht and the trip takes just over an hour.

On arriving, take a *samlor* to the Mekong where there are restaurants and a fine view from the **Nong Khai Boundary Post.** Small river boats ferry locals, and foreigners thoughtful enough to have acquired a visa beforehand in Bangkok, across the majestic Mekong to Tha Deua on the Lao bank, fare 30 baht. The border is open from 8:30 to 11:30 am, and 2 to 4:30 pm, and is closed on Sundays. Signs barring the carrying of guns into premises are everywhere.

The best of the riverside restaurants is the **Udomrod** (℃ (042) 412561), immediately to the left of the frontier post. The little menu proudly proclaims 'Mekong River fish you eat today slept last night in the bottom of the Mekong River'.

From **Wat Haisok**, half a mile away up-river, you can take an hour-long river trip for 20 baht; departure is from the floating restaurant at 5pm daily.

The best hotel in Nong Khai is the **Phanthavy** (℃ (042) 411568-9; 51 rooms; rates: moderate). **Northeast Business and Travel** claim to arrange visas for Laos, valid for 15 days, in five to seven days; they post your passport to the Lao Embassy in Bangkok and charge you 2,500 baht.

And at the full moon in June, the **Rocket Festival** — Bun Bang Fai — is celebrated at Wat Po Chai, next to the bus station.

Wat Kak

This extraordinary Hindu-Buddhist garden is a fifteen minute drive from Nong

Khai. A motorbike bus will take you there and wait to bring you back.

To the sound of the latest Thai pop successes, gigantic mythological figures gesticulate in impeturbable magnificence against the blazing sky. The effect is quite extraordinary, and unique (though there is another such garden at Tha Deua on the Lao side). It is all the work of followers of the local yogi-priest-shaman Luang Pu Buenleuca-Surirat and was begun in 1978. Additional figures, made

from wire, brick and concrete, are being constructed on all sides.

LOEI

West of here is the province of Loei, chiefly celebrated for being the only place in Thailand ever to record frost. It's a mountainous, remote and beautiful region that would repay the attentions of the adventurous traveler. TAT do produce a leaflet on it, but they currently have few takers. You might begin your explorations with the **Phu Kradung National Park**, a lush plateau at an elevation of 1,325 m (4,350 ft), with accommodation available. But you *must* check with TAT before going as the park is frequently and inexplicably closed for extended periods.

WAT THAT PHANOM AND SURIN

In the far east of the region, **Wat That Phanom**, 50 km (32 miles) from **Nakhon**

Phanom, has a huge *chedi* that is famous all over the country. And back in the south, **Surin** has an annual **Elephant Round-Up** in November, organized by TAT. It may seem a tourist-oriented show to some, but the people handling the animals are professionals who are with them permanently. "Elephant football", only one item in a two-day event, is a typical example of the ingenuous Thai sense of humor.

MONSOON COUNTRY

Valuable adjuncts to any trip to the North-East, and indeed to any trip to Thailand, are the books of Thai author Pira Sudham. He was born of peasant parents in Esarn and, with the help of a string of scholarships, studied first in Bangkok, then in New Zealand and London. Writing in English, his two little books of short stories — *People of Esarn* (1983) and *Siamese Drama* (1987) — tell of the agonies of poor country people going to work in Bangkok. His full-length novel, *Monsoon Country* (1987), tells what is virtually his own life story.

It so happens that this author organizes weekend trips for small groups to his home village in Buri Ram Province. He drives the parties himself in a mini-bus or his own car, and the tours include a visit to the Khmer remains at Phanom Rung. Accommodation is in his own house in the village of Napo.

These private tours offer an excellent insight into northeastern village life. For further details, contact the author via G.P.O. Box 1534, Bangkok 10501, or phone him direct on Bangkok (258 1975.

ABOVE and OPPOSITE: Khmer ruins at Phimai. Thailand's northeast has been profoundly influenced by the culture of the Khmers, the people whose great empire, based in modern Cambodia, once dominated the region.

Lastly...

A Genial
Insouciance

A GENIAL INSOUCIANCE

As recently as the mid-eighties, Relax Bay on Phuket was a mysterious little hide-away accessible only by motorbike from Patong. You bumped down the sandy road, past strange talismans nailed to trees, to find a perfect beach on which the blue sea broke in near-silence. Palms nodded, and under them an aging *farang* slept in a faded deck chair, a worn paperback open on his knee. Somewhere in the shadows a Thai in a *sarong* raised an eyebrow to ask if he could fix you a drink. A swing creaked. This, you felt, was the ultimate entranced place, magically seductive, if a bit spooky after dark.

Now, all that has been swept away. The place is today dominated by the Meridien Phuket, with sunbathing on "the white sands of your own private beach". For better, for worse, the world is moving on, and Thailand with it. In far-away Pattaya, oriental lookalikes are prancing to the music of the hit numbers of Madonna, Michael Jackson, and Cher.

The Thais are enthusiastic participators in the modern world. This shows itself in the shining new stereos in the buses and the astonishingly eclectic architecture being put up by the new bourgeoisie (such as the white gothic of Suan Phlu Gardens, near the Immigration Office on Bangkok's Soi Suan Phlu).

But for all the plastic-and-neon aesthetic that characterizes so much of urban Thailand, not to mention the ubiquitous manifestations of the international Snoopy culture, the inescapable charm of old Thailand almost everywhere somehow manages to prevail.

In a country of holy caves and night-markets, there's hardly a subterranean Buddha, a tuk tuk or an open-air food stall, let alone a picture of old King Chulalongkorn, that isn't draped in that most loved of all Thai decorations, a string of fairy lights. And in the early hours boys who in the daytime sell the strings of honey-scented jasmine buds that drivers everywhere hang inside their vehicles emerge, like phantoms from the darkness, to sell roses wrapped in banana leaves to late-night lovers.

And of course it's the Thais themselves that are the real delight. There can be few nations on earth where the people are so extensively amiable, gentle and long-suffering. For someone to come up and ask if they can help you is the most ordinary thing in the world. And everywhere there

is the same genial softness, whatever hardships and deprivations it is covering.

Among themselves the Thais are immensely gregarious. Students or city workers on a brief holiday at the beach sleep together in piles on the floor, and they find it very difficult to believe that anyone is by choice alone. If you tell them that that's indeed what you are, their response is invariably "I'm sorry".

This is connected with the extraordinary lack of solemnity in Thai affairs. Life is to be enjoyed, and this is most easily

Dreams of another life – OPPOSITE: cooling off in Bangkok; ABOVE a pedicab driver – he will spend the night curled up in his vehicle.

done by taking it easy, and giving the beautiful things in life time to bloom.

An abbot lies in state in his temple. The flowers around his coffin are illuminated by pink neon, and outside children fly their kites, and a radio plays the newest love songs in the late sunlit afternoon.

STREET THEATER

A narrow soi is crowded with chairs. The

two-story wooden houses, some with elegant balconies, face each other across the audience, and a stage has been set up at the end of the lane.

Behind the spectators, a Chinese temple's lit up, while at the far end of the soi a film is being projected onto a screen that fills the entire width of the alley. In a brilliant stroke of invention, the screen is so arranged that the audience can watch the film from either side.

The film is well under way when the theater play begins. Boys with heavily made-up eyes and dressed in period glitter (but with modern watches still in place) make slow ritual movements to a basic musical accompaniment. The two musicians sit at the side of the stage, one playing drums, the other a wooden xylophone. Lighting consists of neon tubes and large undirectional bulbs.

The audience keeps up a perpetual chatter throughout, though some people watch and listen with close attention.

Children swing from the edge of the stage.

It isn't long before a comic interlude takes over the show. In a manner reminiscent of Hamlet's complaints about the liberties taken by actors, the performers improvise at inordinate length in increasingly bawdy fashion. The love scenes consist of women trying to inveigle themselves into the company of a particular man and being rudely repulsed. This scenario quickly descends into obscenely erotic horseplay, and the five-year-olds in the audience squeal with laughter at the mock copulations.

A ritual knife-fight ensues — but the final impression is made up less of the songs and music, the fights and slap-stick farce of the play than of the elements of the scene in the soi itself this hot Bangkok night — the crowds of people, the smell of the drains, the light breeze, the TVs flickering in the houses, the percussive music, the actors shouting into their microphones, the children with pink sausage-shaped balloons tied round their heads.

This is *likee*, the popular Thai traveling theater. It's almost impossible to discover it except by following the crowds down some poorly lit back-street to where the light spills off from the stage onto a mass of upturned faces. If you do discover one, sit down and enjoy it. No one will mind – indeed, the humble audience will be honored that you've come. It's a spectacle very close to the heart of Thailand.

ABOVE AND OPPOSITE: ancient modern mix easily in the carefree, relaxed ambiance of the popular Thai street theater.

Travelers'
Tips

VISAS

Your passport must be valid for at least six months beyond your intended period of stay in Thailand.

If you arrive at the airport or frontier without a visa, you will be allowed a two week stay in the country. This may, if you're lucky, be extended once only for a further seven days.

For a longer stay, you need to obtain a visa in advance from a Thai consulate. These are usually processed within 48 hours.

Most visitors will opt for a Tourist Visa. This is valid for 60 days, officially renewable once for a further 30 days when you are inside Thailand. In practice, further renewals are usually possible. Fees for Tourist Visas are the equivalent of 500 baht for the initial visa, and 500 baht for each extension.

If you are going to Thailand on business, you can apply for a Non-Immigrant Visa, valid for 90 days. A letter from a company, organization or institution guaranteeing your repatriation must be included with your application.

Thirdly, Transit Visas are available, valid for 30 days, theoretically for people "traveling in transit through the Kingdom to other countries."

All visas must be taken up within 90 days of their being issued.

The Immigration Office in Bangkok, for visa renewals, is on Soi Suan Phlu, off Sathorn Tai Road. There are also offices in other major centers such as Pattaya and Phuket.

CUSTOMS ALLOWANCES

Foreign visitors may bring in unlimited amounts of foreign currency, but need to declare a total value of more than US$10,000. On leaving the country, an amount over US$10,000 must again be declared, and in this case you will only be allowed to take out a sum equivalent to that which you brought in.

Foreign visitors can only bring in 2,000 baht (4,000 for a family traveling together on one passport), they may only take out 500 baht (1,000 for a family traveling together on one passport).

It is forbidden to bring into the country narcotics (e.g marijuana, hemp, opium, cocaine, morphine, heroin), obscene literature or pictures, and firearms or ammunition unless a permit has been obtained from the Police Department or the "local Registration Office".

CURRENCY

Thai baht come in banknotes of 500, 100, 50, 20, and 10. Coins come in 1 and 5 baht. New coins are being introduced and are currently circulating alongside the old ones.

The baht is subdivided into 100 stang. There are coins for 50 and 25 stang.

BANKS

Thailand's banks are open 8:30 am to 3:30 pm, Mondays to Fridays. They're closed on Saturdays.

The **Thai Farmers Bank** has branches all over the country. Its head office at 400 Phahon Yothin Road, Bangkok 10400, (270 1122 and 270 1133, telex: 81159 FARMERS TH. They have overseas offices in London, Hamburg, New York and Los Angeles.

The **Bangkok Bank**'s headquarters are at 333 Silom Road, Bangkok 10500, (234-3333. Telex: 82638 BKBANK TH. Their overseas branches are in Hamburg, Hong Kong, Jakarta, London, Los Angeles, New York, Osaka, Singapore, Taipei and Tokyo.

IN FROM THE AIRPORT

Bangkok's new International Airport, Don Muang, is a great improvement on the quaint but increasingly inappropriate old one. There's a Tourist Information Office run by TAT, and, of course, a Customs and Excise. Try to avoid extended contact with the latter: it may be full of peasants pleading against levies on tattered carrier-bags full of vegetables, but, as a foreigner, you are automatically bigger game.

Taxi fares into Bangkok are now fixed to prevent overcharging. Go to a central desk and you'll be given a slip of paper with your destination in Thai and the fare written

on it. The fare to central Bangkok will be about 170 baht.

Many arriving visitors looking for transport into Bangkok settle for the "limousine", actually a ten-seater mini-bus run by Thai International. They call at the hotels the passengers ask for in an order decided by the driver. The fare is 100 baht. You will be offered more expensive transportation by the same office, but if you say you want the 100 baht limousine, that's what you'll get. You may have to wait ten or fifteen minutes for the vehicle to fill up.

It's almost as easy to catch an ordinary Bangkok bus (number 29) on the motorway outside the airport, and then get a taxi

in Bangkok to your ultimate destination. The bus costs two baht and will give you an instant taste of Thai life at the grassroots. You'll almost certainly have to stand for the 25 km into town.

CAR HIRE

Touring Thailand in a rented car is a good way of seeing the country. You'll need an International Driving Licence, and then you can rent cars from, among others, the following companies.

In Bangkok: **Avis Rent A Car**, 16/23 North Sathorn Road, (233 0397; **Hertz International Co. Ltd.,** 1598 New Phetburi Road, (252 4903-6.

In Chiang Mai: **Avis Rent A Car**, c/o Dusit Inn Hotel, 122 Chang Khlan Road, ((053) 251034, 236835; Friend's Service, 145 Chang Khlan Road, ((053) 233026.

In Phuket: **Phuket Car Center**, Takuapa Road, ((076) 212671-3; **Pure Car Rent**, 75 Ratsada Road, ((076) 211002.

HEALTH

There are no obligatory vaccinations required for entry into Thailand, other than for Yellow Fever if you have been in an infected area during the previous six days. It's a good idea, though, to consult your doctor, and to have an anti-tetanus injection anyway before leaving home.

Malaria is a real danger, however. It's now on the increase as resistant strains develop worldwide. Koh Samet, for instance, only two and a half hours from Bangkok, is in a malarial area. You should therefore take prophylactic tablets from before you leave home until several weeks after you leave a danger area — to all intents and purposes the whole of Thailand. Your doctor should have up-to-date information on the most effective brands. It's also sensible to sleep under a mosquito

ABOVE: Ready for anything – Thai police in dress uniform.

net where your accommodation hasn't got anti-mosquito mesh over the windows, to burn mosquito coils during the night, and to put repellent on exposed skin from late afternoon onwards. Note that mosquitoes begin to bite well before dark.

But your main enemy is probably the sun. Get into the habit of wearing a hat, avoid sun-bathing in the middle of the day, and only lie on the beach for short periods during your first few days. Sun-tan oils with a high protection factor will help, but better is simply to find your own tolerance levels, and not expect to look as if you've been there a month after your first afternoon.

If you do get seriously ill, contact the Bangkok Nursing Home (℡ 233 2610-9) or the Seventh Day Adventist Hospital in Bangkok, or the Lanna Hospital in Chiang Mai. Otherwise, go to the best hotel near you and ask to see a doctor.

Minor cuts should be attended to promptly as they will become infected very quickly in this climate. Even mosquito bites tend to become septic almost as a matter of course. Hydrogen peroxide solution and basic antiseptics are widely available and you should carry one of each around with you for these, and other minor abrasions.

Lastly, anyone with professional medical knowledge traveling in Asia will want to carry with him a private medical kit for first aid to the cases of often horrific skin disease he will inevitably encounter.

CLOTHING

It's going to be hot, sometimes very hot, so make sure you bring light-weight things with you. Remember that 100 percent cotton is coolest. You will only need anything more up in the north between, say, November and January, when it does get cool at night. Of course, clothes are so cheap in Thailand it isn't really necessary to bring anything more other than what you fly out in — you can kit yourself out very nicely

your first day there. You'll certainly lose out financially if you buy a lot of clothes specially for the trip just before you leave home.

One useful tip is that if there's anything that makes you feel hot all over when temperatures are high it's hot feet. Try wearing soft shoes or sandals, and no socks — you'll be astonished at the difference it makes.

As for decorum, and doing as the Thais do when in Thailand, you'll notice that few adults, other than manual workers, wear shorts in the cities, unless, of course, they're off jogging at sundown in Lumpini Park. Innumerable tourists do, though, and nobody seems to mind — but of course no foreigner has ever succeeded in knowing what a Thai is *really* thinking.

TRAVELING CONDITIONS

Traveling is remarkably painless in Thailand.

Flying within the country is remarkably good value. Thai Airways offer a **Discover Thailand Fare** on its domestic routes — you buy coupons which you then exchange for tickets at what is a bargain rate. As this is meant to encourage foreign visitors to see more of the country, this fare is conditional on your holding international tickets to or via Thailand. Price at the time of writing is US$199 for four coupons — the minimum number you can buy.

Trains and buses are comfortable, they run on time and are very rarely double-booked. The ordinary long-distance buses, with their plastic flowers, shining new cassette players, whirring fans, stainless steel interiors, and food and drink-sellers visiting at every major halt, are a joy. The air-conditioned buses are less colorful but obviously more comfortable, but you should try the ordinary kind at least once. You may well become addicted to them. Enquire, too, about the **Thailand Rail Pass**.

In the country, Thais rarely travel by road after dark. In compensation, the buses begin very early in the morning, frequently at, or even before, first light.

There's only one set-back — as in most Asian countries, safety precautions leave something to be desired. In the poorer areas such as the north-east, accidents due to old and unmaintained vehicles are unfortunately not rare, and in multiple-occupancy taxis — where you may have no alternative but to occupy the passenger seat — seat-belts are unknown.

ACCOMMODATION

The best Thai hotels are excellent and can be judged by the most exacting international standards. Their prices, however, will come as a pleasant surprise. Hotels in the "average and above" category will differ little from those marked as "expensive". They will perhaps have one or two restaurants instead of four, and a more limited range of sports facilities.

Accomodation in the "moderate" bracket ranges from comfortable, Western-style hotels in areas where international tourism has yet to make an impact to the simpler hotels in Bangkok, some of whose rooms may not have air-conditioning or hot water.

Places in the "inexpensive" category can be anything from an idyllic wooden chalet literally on the beach in Koh Samui to a plain, commercial-travelers' hotel up-country in Mai Hong Son or Chiang Saen. This is the category in which there's the greatest range, and where you can never quite be sure what you'll find. Inclusion in this book, however, guarantees certain minimum standards.

The rates for hotels in the body of the text are based on the price of an average double room. Equivalents are:

Inexpensive: under 300 baht (US$12)
Moderate: 300 to 1,000 baht. (US$12 to $40)
Average and above: 800 to 1,800 baht (US$40 to $80)

Expensive: 1,800 baht and over (US$80 and over)

SECURITY

All southeast Asian hotels make special security provision for valuables, for which no charge is ever made. The reason for this is that it is in the hotel's interest that temptation is not placed in the way of its employees. Cash that a Westerner might leave round his room without a second thought could easily represent wealth a room-boy might have to work months, if not years, to accumulate. Accusations and subsequent investigations can do nothing but harm to a hotel which, though anxious to acquire your money, has no interest whatsoever in any of its minor employees doing so.

MAIL

Thai postal rates at the time of going to press are as follows:

To Singapore and Malaysia: Postcards 4.85 baht; Letters under 5 g 8.75 baht; Letters under 10 g 9.00 baht

Elsewhere in Asia: Postcards 5.85 baht; Letters under 5 g 9.50 baht; Letters under 10 g 10.50 baht

Europe and Oceania: Postcards 7.20 baht; Letters under 5 g 10.50 baht; Letters under 10 g 12.50 baht

North America: Postcards 8.50 baht; Letters under 5 g 11.50 baht; Letters under 10 g 14.50 baht

South America: Postcards 9.20 baht; Letters under 5 g 12.00 baht; Letters under 10 g 15.50 baht

Africa: Postcards 7.85 baht; Letters under 5 g 11.00 baht; Letters under 10 g 13.50 baht

The main Bangkok Post Office is on New Road, close to the Swan and Oriental hotels. If letters are addressed to you c/o Poste Restante, Bangkok, this is where they will arrive.

The various counters at the General Post Office are all open at different times.

Poste Restante is open from 8 am to 8 pm on weekdays, 8 am to 1 pm Saturdays, Sundays and public holidays. International Express Mail is open 8:30 am to 3 pm weekdays, 9 am to noon Saturdays. For telegrams, the Telegraph Office is open 24 hours.

THE PHONE

Thailand's phone service is improving very fast now. IDD has been set up, and direct-dial calls to other parts of the country are available from public kiosks in some places.

It's always possible to make international calls from the bigger hotels, but usually with a rather hefty surcharge.

Public offices where such surcharges can be avoided are still rather thin on the ground. The place to go in Bangkok is next door to the General Post Office on New Road. At the time of writing, this is the only place in Bangkok (other than in some of the big hotels) where you can phone abroad direct, and therefore for less then the otherwise obligatory three minutes. The service is reasonably efficient and is open 24 hours.

The following are the area codes inside Thailand:

Central Region
Ang Thong 035
Ayutthaya 035
Bangkok 02
Kanchanburi 034
Lopburi 036
Nakorn Pathom 037
Nonthaburi 02
Pathum Thani 02
Phetchaburi 032
Prachuap Khri Khan 032
Prachinburi 037
Rachaburi 032
Samut Prakarn 02
Samut Sakhon 034
Samat Sungkhram 034
Saraburi 036
Sing Buri 036
Suphanburi 035

Eastern
Chachoengsao 038
Chanthaburi 039
Chonburi (including Pattaya) 038
Rayong 038

Northern
Chiang Mai 053
Chiang Rai 054
Kamphaengphet 055
Lampang 054
Lamphun 053
Mae Hong Son 053
Nakhon Sawan 056
Phetchaboon 056
Phayao 054
Phitsanulok 055
Phrae 054
Phichit 056
Sukhothai 055
Tak 055
Uthai Thani 056
Uttaradit 055

North-Eastern
Buriram 044
Chaiyaphum 044
Kalasin 043
Khon Kean 043
Loei 042
Maha Sarakham 043
Nakhon Phanom 042
Nakhon Ratchasima 044
Nong Khai 02
Roi Et 043
Sakon Nakhon 042
Sisaket 045
Surin 045
Ubon Ratchathani 045
Udon Thani 042
Yasothon 045

Southern
Chumphon 077
Hat Yai 074
Krabi 075
Nakhon Sithammarat 075
Narathiwat 073
Pattani 073
Phang Nga 076

Phuket 076
Ranong 077
Satun 074
Songkhla 074
Surat Thani 077
Trang 075
Yala 073

NEWSPAPERS

There are two English-language papers published in Bangkok, the *Bangkok Post* and *The Nation*. There's not a lot to choose between them — indeed, they often carry the identical foreign news stories. Both are available wherever tourists are found, though far from Bangkok they're often a day or so out-of-date.

TV AND RADIO

Television's almost entirely in Thai. There is, though, what purports to be a simultaneous translation of the main evening TV news on one of the radio stations, but the degree of detail you get has been questioned.

There's an all-English radio station, and two hours of Western classical music are put out every week night from 9:30 pm by enthusiasts at Chulalongkorn University. Programs and wavelengths are in the English-language newspapers.

RELIGION

The overwhelming majority of Thais are Buddhists, but there are plenty of other places of worship dotted around the country, mosques in the south, and Christian churches, especially Catholic ones, almost everywhere. Ask at your hotel for details.

TAT

The **Tourism Authority of Thailand** is the government agency responsible for helping tourists and hence increasing tourism into the country. Its central office is at:

Ratchadamnoen Nok Avenue, Bangkok 10100. (2821143-7. Telex: 84194 TATBKK TH; Fax: 280 1744.

TAT also has offices in the following places:
Chiang Mai at 135 Praisani Road, Amphoe Muang, Chiang Mai 50000. ((053) 235334; fax: 252812.
Hat Yai at 1/1 Soi 2 Niphat Uthit 3 Road, Hat Yai, Songkhla 90110. ((074) 243747 and 245986; fax: 245986.
Kanchanaburi at Saeng Chuto Road, Amphoe Muang, Kanchanaburi 71000. ((034) 511200.
Nakhon Ratchasima at 2102-2104 Mittraphap Road, Tambon Nai Muang, Amphoe Muang, Nakhon Ratchasima 30000. ((044) 243427 and 243751; fax: 243427.
Pattaya at 382/1 Beach Road, South Pattaya. ((038) 428750 and 429113; fax: 429113.
Phitsanulok at 209/7-8 Surasi Trade Center, Boromtrailokanat Road, Amphoe Muang, Phiṭsanulok 65000. ((055) 252742-3.
Phuket at 73-75 Phuket Road, Amphoe Muang, Phuket 83000. ((076) 212213 and 211036; fax; 213582.
Surat Thani at 5 Talat Mai Road, Ban Don, Amphoe Muang, Surat Thani 84000. ((077) 282828 and 281828; fax: 282828.

TAT maintain offices abroad in the following cities: Frankfurt, Hong Kong, Kuala Lumpur, London, Los Angeles, New York, Osaka, Paris, Rome, Singapore, Sydney, and Tokyo.

AIRLINES

Bangkok's Don Muang is a major international airport and is on the schedules of a large number of airlines. The following are their telephone numbers in Bangkok:
Aeroflot, (251 0617/251 1223-5
Air Canada, (233 5900-9 ext 11-14
Air France, (233 9477

Air India, (256 9614-9
Airlanka, (236 9292-3
Air New Zealand, (233 5900-9
Alia Royal Jordanian Airline, (236 8609-17/236 0030
Alitalia, (233 4000-1
Aloha Airlines, (252 3520-2
American Airlines, (252 3520-2
American West Airlines, (234 7876-8
Bangladesh Biman, (235 3616-9 ext 25 and 37
British Airways, (236 0038
Burma Airways, (233 3052
CAAC, (235 1880-2
Canadian Airlines, (253 9097-9
Cathay Pacific, (233 6105
China Airlines, (253 5733
Delta Airlines, (234 7876-8
Dragon Air, (254 7468-9
Eastern Airlines, (253 9097-9
Egypt Air, (233 7601-3
Finnair, (251 5012
Garuda Indonesia, (233 0981-2
Gulf Air, (254 7931-4
Hawaiian Airlines, (236 9513-9
Indian Airlines, (233 3890-2
Iraqi Airways, (235 5950-5
Japan Airlines, (233 2440
KLM Royal Dutch Airlines, (235 5155-9
Korean Airlines, (234 9283-9
Kuwait Airways, (251 5855-60
Lao Aviation, (233 3810
Lauda Air, (233 2544/233 2565-6
LOT — Polish Airlines, (235 2223-7
Lufthansa,(234 1350-9
Malaysia Airlines System, (236 4705-9
Northwest Orient Airlines, (253 4822
Pakistan International Airlines, (234-2961-5/234 2352
Pan Am, (251 4521
Philippine Airlines, (233 2350-2
Qantas, (236 0102
Royal Brunei Airlines, (234 0009
Royal Nepal Airlines, (233 3921-4
Sabena, (233 2020-3
SAS Scandinavian Airlines System, (253 8333
Saudi Arabian Airlines, (236 9395-403
Singapore Airlines, (236 0440
Swiss Air, (233 2935-7

Tarom Romanian Air Transport, (253-1681-5
Thai Airways (domestic), (243 3100
Thai International, (233 8310
Trans World Airlines, (233 7290-1
Union de Transport Ariens (UTA), (233-9477
United Airlines, (253 0558-9
Western Airlines, (234 7876-8
Yemenian Yemen Airways, (253 9097-9
The number of **Don Muang International Airport** is (531 0022-59.
Airport Limousine Service — at the airport (277 0111-3; in Bangkok (at the Asia Hotel) (215 0808 Ext 7347
Airport Bus Service — at the airport (523 6121 Ext 138 or 267; in Bangkok (at the Asia Hotel) (215 0808 Ext 7347.

CONSULATES AND EMBASSIES

These are the telephone numbers consulates and embassies in the Thai capital:

Consulates
Bolivia, (214 1501-9
Dominican Republic, (521 0737/ 521-1282
Honduras, (251 2862
Iceland, (249 1300/249 1253
Ireland, (223 0876/233 0304
Jordan, (391 7142
Mexico, (245 1415/245 7820-1
Oman, (236 7385-6
Peru, (233 5910-7/ 233 5993
Senegal, (573 1976/281 6451
Sri Lanka, (251 0803/252 8774-5

Embassies
Argentina, (259 0401-2
Australia, (287 2680
Austria, (286 3011/ 286 3019
Bangladesh, (391 8069-70
Belgium, (233 0840-1
Brazil, (256 6023/ 255 6043
Brunei, (251 5766-8
Bulgaria, (314 3056
Burma, (233 2237/ 234 2258
Canada, (234 1561-8

Chile, (391 8443/ 391 4858
China (PRC), (245 7030-44
Czechoslovakia, (234 1922
Denmark, (286 3930/ 286 3932
Egypt, (253 0160/ 253 8131
Finland, (256 9306-9
France, (234 0950-6
Greece, (252 1686
Hungary, (391 2002-3
India, (258 0300-6
Indonesia, (252 3135-40
Iran, (259 0611-3
Iraq, (278 5225-8
Israel, (252 3131-4
Italy, (286 4844-6
Japan, (252 6151-9
Korea, (234 0723-6
Laos, (286 0010
Malaysia, (286 1390-2
Nepal, (391 7240
Netherlands, (252 6103-5/252 6198-9
New Zealand, (251 8165
Norway, (258 0533
Pakistan, (253 0288-9
Philippines, (259 0139-40
Poland, (258 4112
Portugal, (234 0372
Romania, (251 0280/ 251 2242
Saudi Arabia, (235 0875-8
Singapore, (286 1434/286 2111
Spain, (252 6112/ 252 6368
Sri Lanka, (251 2789/251 8399
Sweden, (234 3891-2/233 0295
Switzerland, (253 0156-60
Turkey, (251 2987-8/ 252 3220
USSR, (234 2012
UK, (253 0191-9
USA, (252 5040-9/ 252 5171-9
Vatican, (211 8709
Vietnam, (251 5838
West Germany, (286 4223-7
Yugoslavia, (391 9090-1

TAX CLEARANCE CERTIFICATES

These can be a problem. Basically, if you have been in the country for over 90 days *within any one calendar year*, if you have

received a Thai work permit, if you have a Certificate of Residence, or if you entered on a Non-Immigrant Visa Class B (Business) and stayed over 14 days, you will need to have a Tax Clearance Certificate before you are allowed to leave the country.

Applications for certificates should be made to the Tax Clearance Sub-Division, Central Operation Division, Revenue Department, 1 Chakrapongse Road, Phranakorn District, Bangkok.

ETIQUETTE

Thailand is a very easy-going country, but there are nonetheless aspects of life where you need to take care not to give offence.

The monarchy is revered by almost all Thais, and for a foreigner to speak ill of members of the royal family is likely to be offensive as well as dangerous. And when the national anthem is played, such as at 8 am and 6 pm in public places under government administration, such as railway stations or city parks, or in the cinema, you should stop talking and stand still.

In temples, dress respectfully. In many temples you will be denied entry into the room where the main Buddha image is kept if you're wearing shorts. You'll also have to take your shoes off to go into this area. Buddha images, even if they're ruined, are considered sacred and you shouldn't climb on them or show lack of respect in any way.

In mosques, men should wear hats, women should be well-covered, wearing slacks or a long skirt, with a long-sleeved blouse buttoned to the neck and a scarf over your hair. Everyone should take their shoes off, and not enter a mosque at all if there's a gathering of any sort taking place.

Don't touch Thais on the head, even children. Don't point your feet at people, and at least make the gesture of trying to keep your head lower than those of people "senior" to you.

You'll notice Thais almost never lose their temper. They'll carry on smiling even when they're feeling like hitting you. Try to go along with this tradition, and conversely understand that a Thai smile is not an absolute indication that all is well — there may be problems still to be resolved.

The Thai form of greeting, the *wai,* is also a gesture of respect. Don't be afraid to try it. Keeping your elbows tucked in, hold your outstretched palms together (as in Christian prayer) and bow slightly with your head to the person you're meeting or parting from. Hold your hands at chest level for a child, at your chin for an equal, by your upper lip for someone senior to you, and at your forehead for a monk, the king or a Buddha image.

Sex may be a national industry in Thailand, but public "displays of affection" aren't considered very tasteful.

Lastly, you're quite likely to be called by a Thai "Mr John" or "Mrs Sally". This is the way the Thais address each other, and in talking to you in the same way they are merely translating their own polite form of address into English.

VOCABULARY

Geographical Terms and Place Names

The following words occur very frequently in place-names and so a knowledge of them will be especially useful to visitors travelling round the country:

Amphoe — district
Amphoe muang — down-town district
Aow — bay
Baan — village
Chedi — stupa, or tower
Doi — peak
Haad — beach
Hin — stone
Khao — mountain
Klong — canal
Koh — island
Laem — cape
Maenam — river
Muang — place
Nakhom — town
Nam — water
Sapan — bridge

Soi — lane
Soon — city center
Thale sap — large lake
Thanon — road
Wat — Buddhist temple

Numbers

Nueng — 1*; sorng* — 2*; saam* — 3*; see* — 4; *haa* — 5; *hok* — 6; *jet* — 7; *paet* — 8; *kau* — 9; *sip* — 10.

Teens are formed by adding the numbers 1 to 9 after 10 (eleven is an exception, as "*et*" is used instead of "*nueng*"). So: *sip et* — 11; *sip sorng* — 12; *sip saam* — 13, and so on. Another exception is twenty — *yee sip*. Then it's straightforward. *Yee sip et* — 21; *yee sip sorng* — 22; *yee sip saam* — 23, and so on. Thirty is *saam sip*, forty is *see sip*, and so on.

The word for "hundred" is "*roi*", neung *roi* — 100; *sorng roi* — 200, and so on.

So 170, for example, is "*nueng roi jet sip*" (one hundred seven ten). And 465 is "*see roi hok sip haa*" (four hundred six ten five).

The word for "thousand" is "*phan*"; *neung phan* — 1,000. 2,483 is therefore "*sorng phan see roi paet sip saam*".

Greetings

Thais very frequently add the words "*khrap*" and "*kha*" to their speech. They are terms of politeness, and you use "*khrap*" if you're a man, "*kha*" if you're a woman. So:

"*sawatdee khrap*" — hello (if you're a man speaking), "*sawatdee kha*" — hello (if you're a woman speaking).

Useful expressions

"*Khorp khun khrap*" — thank you (man speaking), "*khorp khun kha*" — thank you (woman speaking).

These two words are also used alone to mean "yes". So a man saying "yes" says "*khrap*", a woman "*kha*".

And "no" is "*mai khrap*" (man speaking), "*mai kha*" (woman speaking).

A common (and typical) Thai expression is "*mai pen rai*" — "never mind". It's used to cover all kinds of difficulties.

The following phrases might be useful in taxis/tuk-tuks, or on the back of a motorbike:
chaa chaa noi — slow down
trong pai — straight on
liaw sai, kwaa — turn left, right
yut trong nee — stop here
yuu klai nit diaw — very near
yuu klai — far away
khaa rot thau rai — how much is the fare?
thueng ... bork duay — tell me when we get to ....

Other Useful Phrases

farang — foreigner (a seventeenth century corruption of *français,* French);
wan nee — today; *muea waan nee* — yesterday

phrung nee — tomorrow
phaeng pai — very expensive
yai — big
lek — small
thau rai — how much?
praisanee — post office
sataem — stamps; *sorng* — envelopes.

DEPARTURE TAX

This is now 200 baht to foreign destinations and 20 baht to domestic ones.

BELOW: Golden devotion – veneration of a Buddha image on a float in the Silom Parade, Bangkok.

Bibliography

ANON *An Englishman's Siamese Journals 1890-1893* (1895). Reissued by Siam Media International (now Shire Books). Fascinating account of trips upcountry to the north – Chiang Mai, Chiang Saen and Laos. Easily obtainable at Elite Books in Bangkok. Recommended.

AYLWEN, Axel *The Falcon of Siam* (1988). Methuen. A lengthy historical novel, teeming with the exotic of every kind, on the rise to power of the Greek adventurer Constantine Phaulkon in seventeenth century Thailand.

BOONTAWEE, Kampoon *A Child of the Northeast* (1976) DK Books. Set in rural Esarn, this realistic novel offers many insights into pre-war life in the region.

BOWRING, Sir John *The Kingdom and People of Siam* (1856). Oxford in Asia Historical Reprints, 2 vols, 1969. The official account of the country by the British envoy to the court of Rama IV. Based on a very short time in the country, but solid and voluminous nonetheless.

BURUMA, Ian *God's Dust* (1989) Jonathan Cape. Politically aware pieces on several Asian destinations, including a sardonic section on Thailand.

CADET, John *Occidental Adam, Oriental Eve* (1981) Asia Books. Maugham-like stories of modern Thai life by a writer who has spent many years teaching English in Chiang Mai.

COOPER, Robert and Nanthapa *Culture Shock – Thailand* (1982). Times Books International, Singapore. An excellent little guide to the pitfalls awaiting the uninformed foreigner blundering over-confidently into Thailand.

GEDDES, W. R. *Migrants of the Mountains* (1976). Oxford University Press. A survey of the hill-tribes.

IYER, Pico *Video Night in Kathmandu* (1988), Bloomsbury. Brilliant and amusing pieces on travel in SE Asia by this intelligent young writer. Highly recommended.

KEYES, Charles F. *Thailand: Buddhist Kingdom as Modern Nation-State* (1987). Westview Press, Boulder, Colorado & London. An excellent general outline of recent Thai history. The author researched relations between the Thais and the hill-tribes in Mae Hong Son Province.

MAUGHAM, W. Somerset *The Gentleman in the Parlour* (1930). Heinemann, London. An account of a journey from Rangoon in Burma to Haiphong in Vietnam, made in the days when such trips were still possible.

SMITH, Malcolm *A Physicican at the Court of Siam* (1957). Reissued in paperback by OUP, 1982. Partly memoirs of practice as an English court doctor in the early years of this century, partly a reconstruction of palace life during the earlier reigns of kings Mongkut and Chulalongkorn. Absorbingly interesting and crammed with bizarre and hardly credible detail.

SUDHAM, Pira *Siamese Drama* (1983), *People of Esarn* (1987), *Monsoon Country* (1987). All Shire Books, Bangkok. The first two are short pen-portraits of North-Eastern Thais caught up in the metropolitan labyrinth of Bangkok. The last is a novel closely following the author's own experiences as a scholarship boy transplanted from the impoverished North-East to Bangkok, and later London and West Germany. A successor to *Monsoon Country* will deal with life in Thailand during the 1970s.

TETTONI, Luca Invernizzi and WARREN, William *Thai Style* (1988), Asia Books. A sumptuously-produced book that both illustrates the finest in modern Thai styles, notably domestic decor, and comments intelligently on them.

VERAN, G. C. *Fifty Trips Through Siam's Canals* (1979). Editions Duang Kamol. Following these at water level will give you an authentic view of what's left of what was once the "real Bangkok".

WINTLE, Justin *Paradise for Hire* (1984). Secker & Warburg. A novel set in a Bangkok love hotel written by a distinguished British scholar in a moment of surrender which an age of prudence can never retract.

YOUNG, Ernest *The Kingdom of the Yellow Robe* (1898). Reprinted in paperback by OUP, 1982. A comprehensive overview of Thai life in the late nineteenth century. An authoritative work, and a classic of its kind.

Quick Reference A–Z Guide
to Places and Topics of Interest with Listed Accommodation, Restaurants and Useful Telephone Numbers